Thanks: Giving and Receiving Gratitude for America's Troops

Thanks: Giving and Receiving Gratitude for America's Troops

A Soldier's Stories, A Veteran's Confessions, and A Pastor's Reflections

by Edgar S. Welty, Jr.
Foreword by Uwe Siemon-Netto

RESOURCE *Publications* • Eugene, Oregon

THANKS: GIVING AND RECEIVING GRATITUDE
FOR AMERICA'S TROOPS
A Soldier's Stories, A Veteran's Confessions, and A Pastor's Reflections

Copyright © 2015 Edgar S. Welty, Jr. All rights reserved. Except for brief quotations in critical publications or reviews, no part of this book may be reproduced in any manner without prior written permission from the publisher. Write: Permissions, Wipf and Stock Publishers, 199 W. 8th Ave., Suite 3, Eugene, OR 97401.

Resource Publications
An Imprint of Wipf and Stock Publishers
199 W. 8th Ave., Suite 3
Eugene, OR 97401

www.wipfandstock.com

ISBN 13: 978-1-4982-2063-7

Manufactured in the U.S.A.

Dedicated to My Family
June 2014

The Reverend Edgar Shirley Welty, Sr.
Petty Officer 2nd Class, US Navy WWII, Pacific Theater
24 June 1912–27 January 1985
Minister of the Word, National Association of
Congregational Christian Churches
Founder: Panamerican Institute
Tijuana, Baja Calif. Mexico
Married 2 Oct 1938 to:

Marguerite Elizabeth (Turner) Welty (Betty)
26 May 1918–4 June 2001
San Diego County Ranking Official
A Presbyterian Elder
Mother to:

Marguerite (Ruth) Elizabeth Welty Butner (Margo)
Born: 9 Aug 1942, A Reformed Jew

Roberta Ethlyn Welty (Berti)
Born: 15 Aug 1945, A Unitarian Universalist

Elaine Jacquelyn Welty Hill (Jackie)
Born: 26 May 1949, An Evangelical Christian

& Myself
Rev. Edgar Shirley Welty, Jr.
Born 3 October 1950, A Minister of the United Church of Christ

Rev. Edgar Shirley Welty, Jr.: Author

Contents

Pictures and Illustrations · ix
Foreword by Uwe Siemon-Netto · xi
Preface · xv
Introduction: Simon's Service—Going the Extra Mile · xvii

Part One: The Case for Thanking

1   G.I. Gratitude · 3
2   Confronting Evil · 11
3   Force Against Evil · 14

Part Two: A Soldier's Stories

4   Facing Death · 19
5   My "Basic" Job · 21
6   Close Calls and Stories · 25
7   Cold Warrior · 27
8   An Example of Uncommon Courage
9   A Letter Home · 33

Part Three: A Veteran's Confessions

10   Hidden Wounds · 39
11   Before My Service · 40
12   In Basic Training · 42
13   On Post · 43
14   As a Veteran · 52

Part Four: A Pastor's Reflections
- 15   On Method · 57
- 16   Issues · 71
- 17   City on a Hill · 76
- 18   God and America's Early History · 79
- 19   Religion at the Time of Our Nation's Birth · 81

Conclusion
- 20   What Would God Have Us Do? · 89
- 21   A Final Word · 90

Postscript · 91
Appendix · 105
Resources · 109
Index · 117

Pictures and Illustrations

National Cemetery, Presidio, San Francisco · xxi
Edgar Welty: Soldier · 17
View Over Berlin Wall · 28
Members of the German Democratican Republican Army · 29
Rev. Edgar Shirley Welty, Jr.: Veteran · 37
Frog Vase · 48
Rev. Edgar Shirley Welty, Jr.: Pastor · 55
United University Church · 60
Bas-relief · 61
Two Kneeling Angels · 61
On the Altar; A Single Rose · 61
Stained Glass Picture Window; Santa Barbara · 62
God of Light vs. the Darkness: *Good and Evil* · 63
God in Three Persons: *A Core Christian Concept, The Next Level of Triangle* · 64
Partial Summaries of God: *The Gray Triangles* · 65
The Wheel of Life: *God Ever-Present in Our Life Cycle* · 66
Human Creativity: *God Within Human Effort* · 67
Slices of Reality: *God in Nature; Human Bodies, Minds and Spirits* · 68
A Complex God · 68
Rev. Edgar Shirley Welty, Sr · 71
San Francisco "A City on Some Hills · 81

Foreword

Gratitude, too, is a divine calling

EDGAR SHIRLEY WELTY, JR. is a minister in the United Church of Christ, a Reformed denomination. He has also served two Lutheran parishes as a pastor, and this, I posit, is reflected in the present book. For one of the most compelling Lutheran doctrines holds that every Christian has a divine calling to serve his neighbors in all his worldly endeavors. If he does so in a spirit of love, Luther said, the Christian renders the highest possible service to God and is therefore a member of the universal priesthood in his secular realm where he reigns in a hidden way through his masks, namely us.

"Glorious works He does through us," Luther exulted in his commentary on Gen 29:1–31, explaining man's many divine vocations, "all completely secular and heathenish works."[1] By that Luther meant any of the tens of thousands of callings in the temporal realm, from milking cows and plowing fields to performing household chores and raising children, from learning, teaching, engineering, and doing research, from governing communities and nations to fighting wars on behalf of a government that owes its authority to God (Romans 13). In his treatise, *Whether Soldiers, Too, Can Be Saved*,[2] Luther compared the combatant's chores

---

1. Jaroslav Pelikan and Helmut T. Lehmann, eds., *Luther's Works*, American Edition (St. Louis, MO: Concordia Publishing House, 1955), 5:266ff. Hereafter *LW*.

2. *LW*, 46:93–137.

Foreword

with those of surgeons.³ He went on, "In the same way I think of a soldier fulfilling his office by punishing the wicked, killing the wicked, and creating so much misery, it seems an un-Christian work completely contrary to Christian love. But when I think how it protects the good and keeps and preserves wife and child, house and farm, property and honor and peace, then I see how precious and godly this work is; and I observe that it amputates a leg or a hand, so that the whole body may not perish."⁴

In the summer of 1987, I was a middle-aged seminary student fulfilling my Clinical Pastoral Education requirement at the VA Hospital Center in St. Cloud, Minnesota. I asked to work as a chaplain intern primarily with Vietnam Veterans, because I had covered the Vietnam War as a staff correspondent of West German newspapers over a period of five years. I had accompanied U.S. soldiers into combat. I had been with them when they were wounded or killed. Yes, there were dysfunctional units like the platoon led by Lt. William Calley that slaughtered unarmed civilians in My Lai, but such units ere not representative of the mass of American military men in Vietnam. Luther had harsh words for rowdy killers such as Calley's:

> There are some who abuse this office [of a soldier], and strike and kill needlessly simply because they want to. But that is the fault of the persons, not of the office.... They are like mad physicians who would needlessly amputate a healthy hand just because they wanted to.⁵

Half millennium ago, then, Luther described precisely what happened in Vietnam in the nineteen sixties. Many times I saw GIs risking and often sacrificing their lives to protect civilians. I was with them when they chased Vietcong fighters who by massacring entire families had executed a well-defined strategy of a totalitarian regime. Almost all the soldiers I accompanied into combat exercised their "office," as Luther called it, in a manner that

3. *LW*, 46:96.
4. *LW*, 96.
5. *LW*, 97.

Foreword

was "godly and as needful and useful to the world as eating and drinking or any other work."

Then my editors posted me to New York and Washington. At virtually every fancy cocktail party I attended in these cities I heard the cliché: "Vietnam veterans, my least favorite minority." Across the country, I covered huge demonstrations of young Americans chanting "Ho-Ho-Ho-Chi-Minh," and waving the Vietcong flag: red and blue with a yellow star in the center. This banner was as offensive to me as the swastika was to those who witnessed Nazi atrocities in Germany, for it reminded me of the bodies of hundreds of women and children in a mass grave in Hué, all slaughtered because they belonged to a class that could not be expected to welcome a Communist revolution.

The veterans I ministered too told me even worse stories: Every one of them was accosted as a baby killer, usually by women, within the first twenty-four hours after their return home. Most of these former soldiers in my pastoral care groups had lost their wives or girlfriends to the self-serving pacifist zeitgeist. One was even kicked out of the church he was baptized and confirmed in. "Before you come back, get yourself some civilian clothes and wait until your hair has outgrown your crew cut," his pastor shouted at him from the pulpit.[6]

Now, by Luther's light, if these cruel and self-righteous peace activists were Christians they, too, had divine vocations, which they did not fulfill because they were not looking "at the office of the soldier . . . with the eyes of an adult," as Luther phrased it.

They were U.S. citizens and therefore voters, and as voters they were the sovereigns of this republic. As sovereigns they were called to inform themselves well before taking any civic action, and this means: inform themselves thoroughly about who these Vietnam Veterans were, why and by whom they were sent to Vietnam, and how they conducted themselves there. As sovereigns, too, it was their vocation to give thanks to their soldiers—yes, their

---

6. q.v., Siemon-Netto, Uwe. The Acquittal of God: A Theology for Vietnam Veterans (Eugene, OR: Wipf and Stock, 2008).

xiii

Foreword

soldiers—for sacrificing so much in the Vietnamese jungles and rice paddies.

By the logic of the Lutheran doctrine of vocation the veterans, too, have important callings: to lovingly serve their neighbors by informing them about their experiences, but also, as an act of neighborly love, accept the gratitude they received from those who did not reject them, most likely a majority of their fellow citizens. I leave it to Rev. Welty to tell us the rest of the story, but in the same manner Luther taught us that soldiers, too, can be saved, let me be adamant: They deserve our gratitude. And gratitude, too, is a vocation instituted by God.

—Uwe Siemon-Netto

Preface

THIS IS A BOOK about faith and moral issues facing America's troops. As someone who spent four years wearing US Army Uniforms I have plenty of my "Soldier's Stories." But I don't start my book with these.

Instead I introduce my work with the telling of Simon's service when he carried the cross of our Lord, Jesus Christ. I argue that "Service" is the same as Jesus' call to: "Go an 'Extra' or 'Second' mile." I further argue that Americans are called by Jesus, God incarnate, and common decency to "walk" a "Second Mile," for America's troops and veterans. Finally I argue that this is necessary because troops and vets are in trouble as demonstrated by things as their suicide rates.

This sets up Part One "The Case for Thanking." Part Two relates my "Soldier's Stories." Part Three called, "A Veteran's Confessions" records my stories which could never be told by an Army Recruiter but deal with life as it is the service and the before and after context of my time in uniform. Part Four is my "Reflections" as "A Pastor."

My Conclusion asks the question, "What Would God Have Us Do? And partially answers that question with, "Avoiding Worshiping the Rate of Return & Ourselves." My "final word" is for veterans in particular, and the public in general.

Introduction

Simon's Service—Going the Extra Mile

Walking With America's Warriors

I TRIED TO GET away but I was swept up by the mob. The crowd surged when Roman soldiers marched out the gate leading from the courtyard of their barracks onto the street. They were leading a man crowned with thorns, who had been flogged almost to death. He was carrying the crossbeam on which he was to be crucified. To my horror, this hapless prisoner fell down in front of me into the filth of the street.

Suddenly I felt the flat of a spear point settle onto my shoulder. I looked around and up the shaft of the spear into the disdainful face of a Roman soldier. He sneered and said,

"Hey slimy 'Black Man,' Pick up that cross beam." The soldier shouted at me over the din of the crowd "This man's half dead we don't want him to die before we can hang him on this cross. Get a move on. We can't wait all day."

To those of you who are reading these words image you are hearing Simon of Cyrene speak.

As a Jew from a distant Roman community, Simon had arrived in Jerusalem to celebrate Passover at "The" temple. Simon's faith required him to celebrate its great festival each year and at least once, in his life, in "The" temple. His city of Cyrene, in Rome's Libya was distant from Judea.

Introduction

Simon had traveled this distance at great effort and expense. His pilgrimage to "The" temple promised to be his only chance to fulfill both a holy obligation and a lifelong dream.

Simon also knew the family portion of Passover would start as that Friday's daylight faded. He needed to finish at the temple, walk back through crowded streets, through a small gate in Jerusalem's walls, then back across the fields to his relatives' farm, all before sundown.

Simon had found himself on the street next to the Roman barracks. Suddenly Pilate's soldiers had appeared leading out a man to be crucified.

Another Simon, who had been renamed Peter, remembered Jesus' teaching about soldiers pressing men into service. Peter had heard Jesus say, "And whoever *presses you into service* to go one mile, go with him two." This term of to *press into service* is the same as in Simon (the cross carrier's) required service

This teaching of Jesus is known as, "Going the Extra or Second Mile." Compulsory service demanded by conquering armies had started with the Persians, continued with the Greeks then the Romans.

In the first century, its most common form involved the demand that residents carry the baggage of Roman soldiers for one mile. Jesus asks his hearers not only to do this resented task, the one mile, but also to carry the enemy warriors' baggage for a second or extra mile.

Christians are called by Jesus to carry the burden of our enemies for an extra mile. (And I do not buy the idea that this was merely a ploy to get enemy soldiers in trouble with their commanders. This was, in my view, an actual command of Jesus and should be understood as such.)

As Americans we are called by common decency, to walk with our warriors in active service, and with our veterans, for that extra mile.

But it is hard for most Americans to even start walking that second mile. Many people, particularly politicians, say they

Introduction

support the troops. But can we support the troops if we are disconnected from them?

Today, in Afganistan, we have been involved in America's longest war.

Our engagement in Iraqi was also drawn out. Yet only one percent of Americans are involved in military service.

What kind of support is America giving her troops? Sacrifice in the form of increased taxes? Of course not! Politicians' children sent into harm's way? Very Few! Lip service? Yes!

Each year as America celebrates Memorial Day, each of us, all of us, need to ask ourselves what kind of support we and our fellow Americans give our troops. Each year, as we the electorate go to the polls; we need to confront politicians, those, who would serve us, the question of real support of our troops. Each time, civilians and those who have never served, come into contact with a member of our armed forces or a veteran, it is appropriate to say, "Thank you for your service."

Most Americans say they support our troops. But is that true? Recently there has been an attempt to balance the federal budget by: decreasing retirement for future military retirees, and by increasing the co-pays at medical facilities for military related patients.

Many American politicians and their supporters aren't walking the first mile with our troops. The mile called for by common decency. But for those who aren't Christian: Why should they heed the call of Jesus to walk an extra mile for troops with whom 99 percent of the public has no direct connection?

First our life-style depends on the world's sea-lanes, which our navy keeps open. Form the time of our nation's founding, our army has fought to secure our freedom.

As we took our place among nations, our Marines were established as a rapid strike force. As the cold war began, our Air Force separated from our army, to guard our skies against Soviet missiles and fighters. In the ongoing war on drugs, the Coast Guard has been key. And yes members of the Coast Guard have been serving

Introduction

overseas in recent wars. Americans need to walk at least a mile for the vital role the military plays in our lives.

And we must not forget veterans. I am a veteran, a disabled veteran. I fell 36 feet off the cargo nets in basic training. When I regained consciousness, I saw a drill sergeant and snapped to attention. He ordered me to take the "At ease" position and sent me to Fort Dix's hospital for evaluation.

Three hours later a medic found me where I had been shoved into a side room and forgotten about. He jerked my little finger into place, as he asked me what had happened.

Then he told me to walk down to X-ray to see if my back was broken!

But my lifelong pain is nothing compared to the servicepeople who get stuffed into a body-bag, shipped home in a box, and lay beneath the sod in our national cemeteries or active duty troops one of whom each day blows their brains out or jumps to their death, or veterans who are three times as likely to kill themselves, as the general population and twice as likely to be homeless.

For troops and veterans, yes, I believe we are called on to walk a mile or two. As a veteran, I confess I'd sure like to be thanked that way.

To advocate for walking those miles: I will tell you further stories form my time in uniform. As a pastor, I started this introduction with a reflection on scripture. I have related the story of Simon' service. I have shown how it relates to Jesus' teaching about the "Second or Extra Mile." I proclaim, as a Christian preacher that the God incarnate, Jesus Christ, calls for us to walk the extra mile for enemy troops. I call for all Americans to do the same for our troops.

National Cemetery, Presidio, San Francisco

PART ONE

The Case for Thanking

1

G.I. Gratitude

A Tradition of Thanks for Service

BEFORE MY FOUR YEARS in the Army, I helped plan a public expression of gratitude for troops in San Diego. After my service ended in 1980, I found myself receiving thanks from the same public event. Recently at another ceremony, I was, once again, thanked for my service. Since Veterans' Day, I've been thinking about contrasts between these two events. I believe these contrasts reveal gaps between the public who want to express gratitude, and veterans who deserve to be thanked.

Before and after my military service, my family, through a civic association planned Fourth of July celebrations. Since the association was in San Diego, we often booked a Navy or Marine Band for the "Fourth." Before my time in uniform, I responded to these patriotic concerts with the general pride of any citizen.

After my time in uniform, I was reminded veterans had a specific role in those military concerts. When the band started playing a "Salute to the Services," I did not recognize the Coast Guard's song. But then, the tunes became more familiar. "Off We Go Into the Wild Blue Yonder . . ." brought a couple of Airmen and or Air Force veterans to their feet. Presently dozens of sailors and ex-salts rose and stood for; "Anchors Aweigh . . ." The tune for "From the Halls of Montezuma . . ." caused a competing crowd to snap to attention. For they were, "Proud to claim the title of United States Marines." When I heard the army's tune, I knew to rise with soldiers and army veterans to the applause of the crowd.

A Generational Gap

Decades later about 2010, I attended a special service for veterans. Out of all of the attendees, only myself and one other man had been in the Armed Forces. The worship leader, in dress blues, was neither in the military or a veteran. He was a member of the Civil Air Patrol wearing the uniform of an honorary rank. People did applaud when we two veterans stood. But it seemed odd that after years of war in Iraq and Afganistan only about 1 percent of that crowd were in the military or veterans.

But that ratio reflects current reality. Representatives of the public, with no connection to the military are saying, "Thank you for your service." We, among the few with those connections, are trying to know how to respond. But this ratio is not the only factor causing gaps between the public, active duty military and veterans.

The first gap is generational. I, born in 1950, was subject to the draft. College classmates served in Vietnam. Only my student deferment and luck in the 1969 lottery kept me out of that war. I, and my generation grew up surrounded by those who had served. My father and my wife's father were WW2 Vets. My wife's uncle and my brother in law served in Korea. My barracks roommate served in 'Nam. Veterans, who stood during that 1980s concert on the "Fourth," in San Diego were older. Thus, there is a generational gap between them, newer veterans, and the public.

Another Gap

The special service for veterans I had attended recently demonstrates a second gap. Geography creates this second gap and adds to the generational one. The recent service occurred in the San Francisco Bay Area. Most of the major military installations in the area have been closed. In the San Diego area, most bases have remained open and more were open in the 1980s. Thus the proximity of the military adds to San Diegans' understanding of those who have served. Today San Francisco area residents rarely rub elbows with the members of the military and few serve.

Two and a half stories flesh out these and other gaps' significance.

The first story demonstrates the gap between those with military experience and those without. In 1980, after my discharge from active service, I stayed in West Germany, working on a post, as a civilian. I happened to walk into an USO office, which provided recreational services. Someone, with no field training, was promoting a "Camping" trip. A servicewoman, who had recently experienced the field during her "Basic training," couldn't see why going into the field, to "Camp," could possibly be fun.

She asked, "Will I have to sleep on the ground?

The saleslady became confused, so I helped this servicewoman to discover the differences between "Camping" with the USO and army field training during "Basic."

Overnight shelter: "Basic" training; The men's "Bivouac" featured sleeping and in turn keeping watch in a two man "Fox hole" with a "Front parapet." The women snapped together "Shelter halves," tenting over two sleeping bags on the ground.

Overnight shelter: USO camping; Heated cabins with four bunk beds in each. Don't have a sleeping bag? The lodge will provide blankets and fresh sheets for a fee.

Sanitary: Basic training; Field latrines, A hole covered with a wooden platform with an attached bottomless box with a hole and sometimes a seat and cover on the top. Hopefully there's still paper on the roll on the nail in one of the poles around which are stretched a canvass privacy screen.

Sanitary: USO camping; We have flush toilets. We aren't uncivilized. But sometimes there's a line for the ladies' restroom.

Bathing: Basic training; Wait in line before meals. Stick your hands under a faucet attached to a "Water buffalo" (a tank on wheels). Wipe you hands on your pants Showers? Wait 'till you get back to the barracks.

Bathing: USO camping; Showers and washbasins are provided. Hot and cold running water, why yes and towels are provided. Heat? Of course the restrooms and cabins are heated. Sorry we have no air-conditioning but summers here are rarely hot.

Food: Basic training; Pick up your "C-Rations" off the truck. Hope those cold cans in the box contain something worth eating. Bad luck? Try working out a trade. Don't worry, with 38 strokes of that little can-opener you'll get at your food.

Food: USO camping; Walk down to the dinning hall. Our menu provides a modest section of hot foods ready for pickup on the food line. Have as much of anything you want. Don't see your favorite selection? Talk to the chef!

The above story demonstrates the way people with and without military experience can speak past each other. A second story narrates the generational gap and introduces other differences in experiences between veterans

One Last Gap

Decades ago, my mother and I paid a visit to an old friend who had checked into a VA hospital. Mom asked, "How are you?" He answered, "I'm here for the duration." Since Mom had been a navy wife, she knew instantly what he meant. I had to recall the terms of WW2 service. Then return home from the military came, after a wound made you unfit for duty, were killed or six months after victory was won. Thus he was telling us he was never going home from the hospital.

Since WW2, most members of the US Armed Forces have known when their deployments, tours and enlistments would end. Many who have served may remember, "Short-Timer Calendars." A draftsman in my engineering unit created a calendar to count down a thousand days. It seemed excessive. His years in Germany would only total 1,095 days. But he wanted to get back to his "World," home, the USA.

G.I. Gratitude

Since gaps between generations affect communication, and geography restricts the exposure of most American communities to military life; how can we bridge these gaps? How can we enhance the ability of the public to meaningfully thank veterans? How can we help veterans to receive gratitude for their service, from other kinds of vets and from the public?

Why Thank

Before we proceed to these questions of, "How"? Let's ask, "Why"?

I believe the public's need to thank active and ex-military members is based on an uncomfortable knowledge. The public knows Americans live in a dangerous world. Our citizens thus agree on the need for our Armed Forces. Our citizens also know America relies on the service of a select few. The vast majority knows it's not their service, which secures our nation. That gives the public a need to properly thank those who do serve.

Why do veterans need help to receive gratitude for their service? The truth is veterans are in trouble. Lets look at one issue, suicide. Twenty-two vets a day are killing themselves. Self-inflicted deaths among veterans are three times the rate as among the general population. How is this real in the world? I found out how, years ago.

The issue became real for me through a series of events. These happened on and around my Army post. I was quartered as a single enlisted man in Smiley Barracks, Karlsruhe, West Germany. I was assigned to Headquarters Company 18th. Engineer Brigade. Other companies, within Smiley, included a military police company.

The MPs policed our barracks, the surrounding installation called Paul Revere Village and other nearby posts. Paul Revere village contained housing and other amenities for army family life. At nearby Gerszewski Barracks, single soldiers were housed for the headquarters and line companies of two of our engineer battalions.

One day, an incident occurred over at Gerszewski. One of our combat engineers went nuts. He picked up an ax, went to headquarters, and started smashing doors and windows. MPs were there shortly but they watched him for a long time. It was Christmas, on the door to the Command Sergeant Major's office was taped a poster of Santa. The ax-man knocked down the wooden door, and then carefully chopped away everything but Santa. Finally, with no more intact doors or windows left, our crazy engineer put down the axe. He then tried, without success, to flip a jeep. The MPs then grabbed him from behind.

I asked myself at the time why did the MPs allow so much property damage. Why didn't they wound, then arrest, the ax man? I found out that the use of deadly force by law enforcement is regulated for good reason. Most police do not even draw their weapons unless they are expecting armed resistance. And if the MPs had used their M1911 pistols, they risked causing death or permanent injury. Note: The M1911 fires a heavy bullet of 45 caliber with a large charge. The weapon was designed to kill or inflict massive injury quickly on charging Moro tribesman in the Philippines in 1911.

There were rumors that Karlruhe's MPs had not always been so cautious. It was said that: One MP attempting an arrest had killed someone instead. With all due respect for the Clint Eastwood's character in "Dirty Harry," the incident did not, "Make," the MP's "Day." Instead I think it was connected to why this MP took his own life.

At first he tried to blow off his head. As he pulled the trigger, he dropped his pistol into his lap and shot himself in the stomach. After hospitalization, he was under watch in his third story barracks room. He got out of bed one morning, went to the window and threw himself out. He might have survived the fall. But his head hit a steel railing and his skull was shattered.

This happened in the mid-morning when I was at work. Hours later, as I walked past the scene on my way to lunch; I tried to resist my morbid curiosity. But I found myself looking for signs of the tragedy. But the post authorities, for the sake of morale, had cleared away all signs of the event.

The Need to Give and Accept Gratitude

This account of suicide brings us back to why veterans need to accept gratitude. It is also one issue key to how to increase public understanding of military life. This first issue is how the act of killing, or preparing to kill, affects our warriors. A second issue is the realities of war. Another issue involves the complexities of military ethics. The fourth issue to be explored is how the probability of success of military missions affects those who fight. I will explore these issues through stories about, confession of and reflections on my experiences with each.

My experiences with the issue of killing started with a larger, encompassing issue. That issue is, "What to do about evil in the world." I've had a long twisting journey with this issue. As a child of the "Cold War," I was marched into my grade school auditorium for yearly showings of two films. One showed the twisted nature of Nazism. Another depicted the nightmare of the "Red" takeover of Russia.

As a pastor's son, I had a "Sunday School" understanding of the benedictional phase of, "Do not return evil for evil." As a preteen, I literally turned the other cheek when slapped in the face. As a young teenager, when I first spent time by myself, I was confronted with the evil of murders at the University of Texas in Austin. As a high school freshman, I defended the Vietnam War using the "Domino theory." As a high school senior, I learned of the horrors of nuclear war at a weeklong "National Security Seminar." As a student in college, I became disenchanted with the "Vietnam War."

The specific issue of killing came into focus for me when I enlisted at the age of twenty-five. I faced the question of "Why do you want to kill/," by a child relative. In "Basic," I found my training prepared me to kill on command. And I have realized, over time, that was my "Basic" job regardless of my "Military Occupational Specialty."

In spite of serving in peacetime, I had near encounters with combat's carnage. Experiences shared by others had added to my knowledge of the realities of war. My "Basic" training in combat ethics was foundational. But reflection while in uniform, activism as a church elder, graduate work as a seminarian and pastoral work as a minister has built on that foundation. In training sessions on post, the probability of success for our unit's mission was clarified. Expanded details of my experiences provide a framework to explore each of these issues.

I have contrasted two ceremonies for Veterans' Day. I have pointed out generational and communication gaps. I have told a story of a soldier's tragic death by his own hand. All this to communicate the need to thanks our troops.

Let us give and receive thanks!

2

Confronting Evil

Learning about Evil

LET ME GO BACK in time. I attended grade school in the second half of the 1950s. Wide concrete walkways with roofs on steel posts connected our classrooms. Twice a year, all classes were formed up outside our classroom doors. Teachers lined us on the concrete walkways, boys to the left and girls to the right. We moved out as classes on our teacher's command towards our lunchroom.

Everyone who had been in our school over half a year knew what was coming. As class after class filed in, we found our lunchroom transformed. Tables and benches were lifted into the walls. Folding chairs had been rolled out on carts from under the stage. Older kids had set up the multipurpose room as an auditorium. A screen was lowered.

One of two movies was about to be shown. The most memorable scene in the film about Nazis involved torches. Flame-bearing storm troopers marched into a nighttime rally. Seen from above massive columns of men bearing flicking torches formed two crossing lines. Then they twisted the cross into a swastika. Many grade-schoolers were bored from many years of this ritual. They registered their protests by marching lock step back to their classrooms.

In another six months, our school would show the other annual film. The topic was the Russian revolution. Its most memorable scene involved mass executions. Prisoners were formed into three lines. In front of them was an open trench. Three men stood along the gap in the earth. Men at the head of the three columns raised rifles. Shots rang out. Men became bodies falling into the trench. The executioners handed the rifles to next man in line and took their place along the trench. As this happened on screen, those who seen the film before whispered, "Watch for the flying hat in the middle!" Sure enough, every time the shots rang out middle the middle hat flew up. And many of us laughed each time.

Our reactions caused our parents and teachers to double-down. Children must learn how Nazism and communism are evil. As for Nazism: Most of our fathers served in WW2 or had friends or relatives who had. The Third Reich's evil was the justification for many sacrifices during the war. As for communism: The Soviet Union's postwar domination of Eastern Europe was seen as their first step in a plan to spread tyranny. Many refugees from the Red Army advances, living in the San Diego area, were rabid anticommunists.

Evidence of WW2's horrors did not just exist in the memories of my parents' generation. As a ten year old, I used war surplus lime to line out our school's baseball diamond. I was spooked to discover instructions in the bag of how to stuff bodies.

The Austin Tower Shootings

When I was sixteen, I was given a scholarship to a weeklong Folk Dance Camp. We learned dances form all over the world. A girl I was madly in love stayed with her mother in a cabin. I slept in an old trailer made of wood provided by the conference center. It was the first time I spent a week all by myself.

Suddenly into this idyllic setting came news of senseless evil. An ex-marine killed both his wife and mother. He then went to the University of Texas in Austin, killed three more people as he climbed its tower. Then from the observation deck shot down at random. He ended up killing 16 and wounding 39, before he, himself, was gunned down.

With that I learned thoroughly that evil can crop up at any time and we must be ready to respond but how?

3

Force Against Evil

Pacifist Aggressive

When I was entering High School, I was confronted by violence on the street.

Two archrival high school football teams had squared off. The home team on home coming night had lost. I cheered on the street next to the football field for my winning team after the game.

Someone became very angry. He jumped out of a car. He got in front of me and slapped me across the face.

As a pastor's son, I had a "Sunday School" understanding of the benedictional phase of, "Do not return evil for evil." So, I literally turned the other cheek. Then the other teenager pulled a knife. I dared him to use if it made him feel good.

Then God intervened. Someone's parent showed up and took me home.

My father took me to the police station to identify my attacker. I stared at young men through one-way-glass. My bravado dissolved. I melted into a puddle of tears. I was dismissed as a worthless son.

Defending the "Domino" Theory

As a high school freshman, I took a course in Public Speaking. I remember two things from that course. First: Since I swayed at the lectern (my Dad did the same thing in the pulpit), my teacher told my classmates to sway every time I did. I was cured in a hurry. Any indication of left to right motion resulted in classmates about falling sideways in their desks. The second thing was my topic. I defended the Vietnam War using the "Domino theory."

Fifty Percent Survival?

During one of my semester breaks in college, I went to the first week of a two-week seminar on National Security. It was held at the Naval Basic Training Facility in San Diego. "Light Birds," that is Lieutenant Colonels from the War College gave six hours of lectures a day with slides to illustrate their points

I must've been an odd sight on base. I had long hair. I wore mustard colored hip hugging cords, a peasant shirt and my sign of the zodiac on a chain around my neck. My shoes were "Penny loafers." But I didn't care how little I fitted in; I was interested in the topics.

One lecture topic I found not only interesting but also appalling. An Air Force Lieutenant Colonel said if we had enough bomb shelters ninety percent of us would not die in an all-out nuclear war only fifty percent would be dead.

"Sticks and Stones" and Other Protests

As a student in college, I went to a one-act play about the Vietnam War. Its basic premise was due to serial exaggeration up the chain of command about the effectiveness of military operations America was fooling herself about the win-ability of the war. This as I recall was called, "Sticks and Stones." In addition to seeing this play critical of our involvement in Vietnam, I found myself attending all sorts of rallies.

Thanks: Giving and Receiving Gratitude for America's Troops

I was a Russian Area Studies major. I found myself speaking against the granting of tenure to a radical professor. He taught a class billed as "Comparative Economics" which never mentioned the USSR. Instead lectures were filled with praise for "Red" China and Cuba.

The hearing was held downtown in San Diego's Federal building. Riot police blocked a basement hallway. I dressed as the Hippy I was, joined two guys from the ROTC to complain.

PART TWO

A Soldier's Stories

4

Facing Death

I HAVE ENCOUNTERED BODIES killed on an urban battlefield. I then lived in South Central Los Angeles. At night I would hear gunfire. Rival gangs were fighting turf wars. Police, in squad cars driving along the streets, in helicopters hovering above, were trying to impose order.

I sometimes saw the bloody results of that disorder. Riding the bus, I arrived late at a transfer point. The police were picking up a body off the bench where I would have been sitting a few minutes earlier. Another time I choose to get off the bus one stop later. A bloody corpse occupied my normal stop. One Sunday morning, I walked through the blood of a drive-by shooting. A car full of gang-bangers had crashed into vehicles stopped at a red light. A rival gang sprayed them with bullets. Blood from their bodies and nuggets of glass from their rear window carpeted the crosswalk behind my church.

I came close to being killed in South Central L.A. One day I walked out of my house and turned towards the store and our driveway. Suddenly a low riding car swooped into my driveway to turn around. I must have shown irritation at my space being invaded and my walk being impeded. One of the young men dressed in the regalia of a major gang leveled a pistol at me. It was a 45 caliber blue nickel plated automatic. I knew the power of such a weapon. I had gone to the range with the army's version. I knew he could take my head off. I figured I had nothing to lose. So I yelled, "F**k yourself!" over and over. The driver turned the low-rider around. He and the gunman drove away.

This wasn't the only time a firearm had been trained on me. During basic training, we had started marksmanship instruction on one rifle range. When we continued our rifle instruction, we were taken to a different range. This unused range was home to deer. The first few shots flushed out several bucks. Trainees with hunting backgrounds cut down the game. A cease-fire order was given. We were told the day before a trainee had shot a drill sergeant. We were told to keep our weapons pointed downrange and fire only on command. If we did not, we could be shot. We saw a sniper in a tower over us.

In Germany, I found myself in a similar situation. Our unit was decommissioned as the 24th Engineer Group. Then we were recommissioned as the 18th Engineer Brigade. The ceremony involved troops from our HQ Company, each of our battalions, and French and West German units. Many civilian and military VIPs attended. We marched in with unloaded slung rifles. We were told if we dropped our weapons on the ground to let them stay there. Snipers in a tower over us would shoot, if anyone made a threatening move.

The reason for this security was the recent assassination of the Attorney General of West Germany. Baader Meinhoff terrorists had gunned down him, his driver, and another official. They had been murdered a few hundred meters outside our front gate. Whenever we went for an extended run in the woods across the street we passed a small flower garden planted on the site. Today a granite monument marks the spot.

5

My "Basic" Job

When I had enlisted in the Army, my nephew asked a question. I, at 25, was still six foot two. He, at eight years old, came up to my chest. He looked up with his little boy brown eyes. He addressed me with a family nickname.

"Uncle Igor," he asked, "Why do you want kill people?"

"What do mean?" I responded.

"You joined the Army that's what they do!"

"Oh, I'm going to be a draftsman and draw plans for buildings." I said.

At basic training I was injured. For safety reasons, on my first trip to the rifle range, I was off the firing line. They sent me instead down into the target pits. There we mounted white cloth targets with black human silhouettes on frames. We hoisted up the targets above grade. A volley of shots rang out. We lowered the targets. On the white bordering areas we pasted black little patches over the bullet holes. Inside the human silhouettes white patches were pasted on black. We raised the targets.

Drill Sergeants with scopes on the firing line kept score. Unaccounted rounds were complete misses. Black patches on white were near misses. Each white patch on the black human silhouettes scored as a hit or a kill.

Thanks: Giving and Receiving Gratitude for America's Troops

It didn't take long to realize that my nephew was right. The Army trains each soldier to kill people. Not all military missions require killing but many do and most all service members must be ready to kill. My time pasting patches on human silhouettes was only the first lesson. My second lesson came when I moved through a firing course shooting human shaped pop-up targets.

Training for killing even continued as I prepared for my non-combat role. My Military Occupational Specialty (MOS) was Construction Draftsman. My Advanced Individual Training (AIT) involved no weapons. But I was called on to perform extra duty. The cash in the Finance Company required guarding over Thanksgiving. The regular guards wanted to spend the holiday with family. Lowly trainees can do that!

I had earned a BA before I enlisted. So the Army granted me rank. By contract I came in as a PFC and became a Specialist 4 in six months. There were six months of delays because I was injured in Basic and because of when my AIT class started. This meant, as a Spec 4, I was Class Leader.

So my Company Commander was surprised, when I volunteered. I had expected to do this guard duty with an M16. But our standard issue rifle was not the best weapon for the confines of the jail cell like Finance Company cage. Shotguns were used.

And we were required to train with those weapons. So I found myself qualifying with a double barrel shotgun. But I did not know how much to brace myself before taking my first shot. The backfire knocked me onto my backside. Word got back to my Company Commander. I became a supernumerary. It was supposed to be an honor. But in my case it meant: Specialist Welty is formally part of the Thanksgiving guard detail. But keep him on standby. Use those who can safely use shotguns!

Friday after Thanksgiving I was at the mess hall having my breakfast. A woman from the guard detail sat down at the table next to me. She told a story about her duty the night before. Robbers had attempted to shoot their way into the Finance Company's cage. She had shot one in the face with both barrels. I moved away.

My "Basic" Job

I wanted to keep my food in my stomach. I did not need to know that she had blown someone's head off!

The call to be ready to kill disturbed me. I was left behind during basic as a barracks orderly. I studied my bible and saw a chaplain. On leave, I went into the Quakers' meeting house in Philadelphia. I walked, in uniform, into a room with William Penn's portrait. Someone I spoke with pointed out that William Penn had been a fine swordsman. In time God had called on Penn to put down his sword to become an early pacifist. I thought, in time, God might call on me to put down my sword.

When I arrived at my permanent post I was issued a weapon's card. When so ordered, I took that card to our company's arms-room. The outer iron grill to the door would be standing open. The top half of the Dutch door would be turned inward. Over a counter built into the door's bottom half, I would hand in my weapon's card. Our company armorer would look at my card and find my assigned rifle. Yearly, I went, with my M16, to the range to maintain my marksmanship. Whenever we went on alert or to the field, I would carry my rifle, the sword of a modern soldier.

I had explained, to my young nephew what I would do in the army. I had said, "I going to draw plans for buildings." I did so through subordinate draftsmen. But we never took our drafting tables into the field. Nor did I take my calculator with which I totaled the amounts of building materials and the costs of construction. Nor did the design officer and I take our engineering manuals we used to write specifications. He holstered his pistol. I slung my rifle.

In the field, we set up our brigade's command post. We left our peacetime role as draftsmen, soil analysts and surveyors. We assumed our wartime role; soldiers patrolling the perimeter of our encampment. My boss, the peacetime design officer, became a combat engineer. His pistol would help to defend the command post at close range

In the field, we rehearsed, "What they do in the army," which is to wage war. A Drill Sergeant, during "Basic," had summarized what war meant for any soldier and me. "You may think it's your job to die for your country. It's your job to make sure some other sucker, (presumably an enemy soldier), dies for his country!" In other words, "What," I as a soldier, could be called on to, "Do in the army," was to "Kill people," (the enemy). My little nephew looking up at his uncle had spoken more truth than I was ready to hear.

6

Close Calls and Stories

As part of Basic training, we lobbed live grenades. I only managed to throw mine a few feet over the low concrete wall on the edge of the range. The Drill sergeant threw me down along the wall. He lay on top of me as the concrete absorbed the blast and fragments. We got up to observe the gaping carter blown into the ground by my grenade. This evidence of the force of a grenade would help me understand an incident during my AIT.

One day, during Advanced Individual Training, we found the back entrance to our mess hall cordoned off. MPs had put up "DO NOT CROSS" tapes all around the office back of the kitchen. The mess sergeant had sat down at his desk. He had opened a package addressed to him. It was a box of grenades triggered to explode. Most of his body was spattered over the white tile walls of his office. The MPs found his booted feet under the desk. His boots were marked with his name and Social Security number.

I was reminded of the utility of regulations regarding the labeling of headgear, belts and footgear. Our drill sergeants had required us to make these markings in Basic. Annual inspectors crosschecked to make sure that task was kept up to date. It's a good idea. Soldiers are often blown apart. When explosions occur, our army needs to sort out which body parts are whose.

Thanks: Giving and Receiving Gratitude for America's Troops

But casualties of war can remain intact. I had developed a relationship of trust with an army buddy. As he started this tale from Vietnam, his eyes fixed into a "Thousand yard stare."

As a firefight ended, he looked towards a soldier at his side. The soldier seemed only to be missing an eye. Then the man's helmet fell off. A bullet had been set spinning end over end as it clipped the eye socket. The brains and the exploded back of his friend's skull fell off with the "Steel Pot" that had been on his head.

Such incidents invoke agony. Why is he or she dead or injured and not I? One can write it off to pure blind bad luck. But what if the living and or injured warrior knows and or believes there was something they should have done? A tale form the Korean War illustrates the anguish such inquiries cause.

One of the allies of the United States caused devastation to enemy morale. They would sneak up on pairs of sleeping sentries. They would kill and decapitate one. They would place the head they had removed on display. The second sentry, upon waking, would confront the gruesome sight.

Such tricks are no doubt ethically questionable. But the story points one of dilemmas of military ethics. It's not just what a warrior does. Often it's what was not done. The sentries in the story had a duty to their comrades in arms to stay alert

We have heard about training to kill. We have described carnage

We have spoken of military ethics Let us thank or be thanked for the facing of those challenges.

7

Cold Warrior

The Warsaw Pact

> *Polyushko, polye; polyusko polye;*
> *Yedoht nasshe gilroee,*
> *Yedoht Sovietsky Armee gilroee*

This is from is a Soviet Army Song, Translated from the Russian: It means roughly:

> *Across the Meadow-lands (or Russian Steppes)*
> *Come our heroes,*
> *Come the Soviet Army heroes*

From early January 1977, until April 21, 1981, I stood ready to help repel an invasion of Soviet Army troops, along with other Warsaw Pact forces, of West Germany.

Let me tell about my experiences doing this; first in Berlin, then at the Fulda Gap and finally in the field as a member of HQ Company of the 18th Engr. Bde.

Thanks: Giving and Receiving Gratitude for America's Troops

In Berlin

I stepped off the train in my forest green, class "A," US Army uniform. Our American Army uniforms   feature a suit coat with brass buttons and epaulets and matching forest green slacks. Under my uniform coat, I wore a regulation poplin tan shirt with a black tie. Over all this was my green overcoat. Under all of it were the top and bottom of my long underwear. A visor hat capped off the look.

Snow lay on the ground one to two meters deep. Giggling kids were throwing snowballs. The artic wolves in the Berlin Zoo were romping for joy. I, born and raised in Sunny Southern California, stepped carefully, in my "Low Quarter" shoes, on icy walkways.

I had earned an educational trip to West and East Berlin when I won a Soldier of the Month competition as a Specialist Four in Headquarters Company. It was 1978 and the "Cold War" was in full sway.

Guides showed us the landmines which lined the "Wall" dividing the city.

Sniper towers were set up to shoot would be escapees from East to West. At "Checkpoint Charlie," we saw a suitcase a East German worker had used to smuggle his wife out. We saw lists of people who had died during mad dashes under or over the wall. We observed photos of dozens of tunnels.

View Over Berlin Wall

On the Eastern side of the wall, we saw units of the German Democratic Republic's Army. They processed around with great ceremony like Nazis without the fashion sense. The Russians, guarding their war memorial, did a slower goose-step.

But the military were not the most memorable characters we encountered.

Members of the German Democratic Republican Army

One was a lone worker, up on scaffolding, repairing a church bombed out over thirty years before in WW2. It was oblivious his communist bosses had little interest in re-opening a house of worship.

The other was a female restroom attendant. When she handed me a towel,

I tipped her in East German Marks. She threw the coins back in my face.

She wanted dollars, West German Marks, Francs, currency that would buy something on the "Black Market"

Fulda Gap

Up on the wall in the mess hall was posted a saying from a Crusade commander.

It read:

"Kill them all! Let God sort them out!"

It seemed an odd motto for an American Tank Battalion. I had driven our officers to an construction site along the Intra-German Border, at the "Fulda Gap," a mountain pass in central Germany, the route of invasions from the East.

Thanks: Giving and Receiving Gratitude for America's Troops

Massed over the fence line, pass the tank traps, were row on row of Soviet Armour. On our side were not nearly as many vehicles. Men in towers on each side watched the other side. There was tension which promised a mad killing spree in case of war. The power that might be released could be felt in the air.

We in the 18th. Engineer Brigade had heard about that possibility.

We, who lived in the enlisted barracks, were billeted beside an American housing area.

It was called Paul Revere Village and in its "Minuteman" theater, we were briefed yearly on the power of the Warsaw Pact.

Army lecturers donned Red Army uniforms and marched in with AK 47s some with 50 round clips, others had 200 round drums.

In The Field

Alerts, official notices everyone must report ready to go out into the field, happened in the wee hours.

When these "Alerts" came down. We would grab our field gear off the top of our wall lockers. There was our web gear, which consisted of a belt and suspenders. On the belt was clipped a canteen, two ammo pouches, a mess kit. On the back of our suspenders we wore a sleeping bag holder. We slung rifles and gas masks. On our heads were helmet liners, with steel pots covered with camouflage covers.

After running doing this, and drawing our weapons, we would form a convoy next to the Gym. Jeeps, ton and a quarter trucks and deuce and a halves would be ready to roll. Then they'd call it off.

When they didn't call it off, when our convoy rolled, we slept in twenty man tents. The women had an eight-woman tent. In winter, these were heated with stoves.

Once I threw a smoking stove out into the snow. It exploded into a column of flames.

Cold Warrior

Army Absurdities

Air Force Corps of Engineers

During my duty in West Germany, I drove officers on military exercises. In the sedan I drove, I overheard an absurd problem our Army Brigade was having with our Air Force counterpart. When we showed up at their bases we faced locked gates. Thus, they were blocking our mission. They were doing this to demonstrate the need for their own "Corps of Enginneers."

Nuclear War Plans

Another absuridity came about when we planned and trainned for nuclear war. We were trainned to hit the ground when a nuclear devise went off. Then we were to count, "One thousand, two thousand, . . . to time the interval between the flash and blast. Then we were to look at the forming musroom cloud. Using our hands: we were to measure, one finger, two finger, . . . whole hand wide. We were to radio that information in. Non-commisioned officers planned to use these reports, maps and weather reports, which detailed wind speed and direction, to plot operations around the likely fallout.

Key personnel were issued badges which registered the accumulated radiation. Pass a certain point, everyone would die! But in the meantime, continue the mission!. We made jokes that in case of nuclear war, we would not have a chance to get off the toliet before we were glowing in the dark, soon to die an agonizing death. And given the imbalance of conventional force in Europe, a tactical nuclear war was likely.

I talked about this to some officers while driving them. They changed the yearly briefings to say we had a chance with a conventional defence.

8

An Example of Uncommon Courage

IN MY ARMY UNIT we were luckier than most. We had no racial strife, but we came close to a riot one night in the barracks. Except for the courage of two homosexuals blacks and whites might have come to blows.

A mostly black platoon had joined with our almost pure white unit. One Saturday night, when a lot of us had drunk a lot of beer, some people wanted to show who was boss. I remember waiting in my room expecting fistfights to break out. In our wide hallway a group of blacks formed at one end. Facing them were whites and the insults were flying back and forth.

Suddenly, out of the doorway between the two groups came the company "Queer" and his partner from the company downstairs. They fluttered in on tiptoe, pleading in high-pitched voices, "Come on boys Let's not fight!" Most everyone laughed and decided not to fight.

I have always thought those men, who made themselves into potential targets, showed uncommon courage.

9

A Letter Home

MAR. 30, 1978

Dear Mother,

    Perhaps I painted too bleak a picture of life here. I do have some barracks friends. George and I have long interesting discussions about philosophy and many subjects; in fact we are almost constant companions. In my room no one smokes cigarettes let alone pot. We like German beer but no one in our tight circle of four has a problem of alcoholism. I have the library and the public parks.

    Probably the reason I struck out so bitterly at the army in my letters to you is that your comments and newspaper clippings showed you were trying to sell me on being a proud part of a professional army. You should know from being a navy wife that the service is a crude place. But today's army is a cruder place than the service was a few years ago. The voluntary concept has meant that most of the people who join the army are immature kids trying to get away from home. Most of these kids come from the lower classes. Fifty percent of today's recruits are high school dropouts. Among the NCOs heavy drinking is the norm. Even the officers are often incompetent and untrained for their assignments. I've seen all of this in a brigade headquarters where the best people are supposed to be kept.

Thanks: Giving and Receiving Gratitude for America's Troops

(Not in original letter: What meant by "A brigade headquarters where the best people are supposed to be kept" is that since our brigade headquarters in-processed all personnel coming into the whole brigade: Two things generally happened; Brigade kept all the women. (Enlisted women in the army are generally brighter and more educated that the men. An assignment to Brigade's' battalions was considered to be a combat assignment. Women are not permitted to serve in combat.) And the brigade gets their pick of the men. However the Master Sergeant in charge of that detail (it turned out) was an alcoholic. But, he was quite clever. He had two hats. He equipped each with our unit's insignia and the pin designating his rank. He placed one on the desk in his private office, so everyone would think he was somewhere in the building. Then he put the other on his head. Then he went to the bar.

My work does give me some satisfaction. By asserting myself, I have gained the reputation of being intelligent and capable of independent thought. My superiors have always gotten the credit for my ideas. But it gives me satisfaction to see some of them go into the design. Two PFCs, and later when I was promoted to Spec. 5, more men, Spec. 4s, were put in my charge, on a project-by-project basis, to create sets of construction drawings. Most respected my authority, I treated my men well, because I knew and they knew that I knew (I told them), that those on detailed to me had more skill at actually putting ink on paper than I would ever master. Note: The women didn't work in the brigade drafting shop, they were assigned to surveying—including one who was a Lesbian. When she had seen enough of Europe she wanted out. She went to her commander and said something like the verbatim below. I heard this from a very reliable source: I think it was from her partner. She told me, this in a bitter tone not an amused one. I think the "Lesbian" in question was leaving not only Europe but also her relationship. I'm straight but I have a gay sister. And "Don't ask; Don't tell" was very informal at that time.

Lesbian (L) comes into officer's (O) office goes up his desk and salutes:

A Letter Home

O: *(In a routine, but firm manner; he had prepared himself for this)* At ease.

L: *(In a serious and dramatic fashion)* Sir, I have something I am required to report.

O: *(In a "So, now it's coming" tone)* Make, your report, Specialist Four X

L: *(In an even more serious and dramatic fashion)* I am a homosexual!!

O: *(Bored)* So what's your point?

L: *(In a desperate tone)* But you have to throw me out.

O: *(In an authoritative tone)* It's at my discretion, you're a good trooper, and I'm keeping you for the full term of your enlistment.

L: *(Snapping to attention, saluting and saying in an amazed and disappointed tone.)* Yes Sir.

O: *(In a matter of fact tone)* Dismissed.

PART THREE

A Veteran's Confessions

10

Hidden Wounds

"It Is What It is"

ENCOUNTER WITH RANDOM VETERAN at Safeway:

> *Observed tired vet carrying an olive green duffle bag in line at the "Deli."*
>
> Ed.: (*Tentatively, politely*) With which branch did you serve?
>
> Vet.: (*With a weary tone*) I served with the SEALS.
>
> Ed.: (*Shocked at the lack of pride, I am confused*)
>
> Vet.: (*With a weary tone explaining*) I was a weapons designer. Some guys went, "Urrah" look at the body count. Some agonized. They told me, "It is what it is."
>
> Ed.: (*Tentatively politely*) I served four years in peacetime. But the first time you shoot at a human shaped target you know, "It is what it is."
>
> Vet.: (*Nods, Awkward pause*)
>
> Ed.: (*Summing up*) Thank you for the insight you've given me.
>
> Vet.: (*Embarrassed, Grunts*)

11

Before My Service

Sloppy Dyslectic

I WAS BORN WITH dyslexia but I did not know I had this learning disability, neither did my teachers.

My fourth grade teacher tried to deal with my, "Bad" handwriting by making me write on the chalkboard one hundred times, "I am sloppy." It just made me angry. My teacher also became angry when I wrote my "hundredth" sentence in a way so nobody could read it.

Spelling was worse. There was a display of rockets on the bulletin board, each one of which went up one notch every time a student got a perfect score on a spelling test. My chubby brown rocket sat in the lower right corner. The rocket of my classmates zoomed pass mine and humiliated me.

Clueless as to my limits, I became a Russian language and Lit Major at California State University in San Diego. Problem is, I can't distinguish between six of the "S" sounds in Russian. (I had even worse problems with Biblical Hebrew. I passed the course literally by kicking someone in the head. But that's a side story.) I was getting straight Cs in my Major and straight As in other courses. So I became a Russian Area Studies Major.

All this was to become a diplomat and do some thing about the nuclear arms race between the U. S. and the Soviet Union. I took the Foreign Service Exam, thought I failed it and joined the Army before I discovered I had passed it

Broken Arm

At thirteen I broke my arm. I was going up to a tree house and a rung on the ladder I had built cracked in half. I fell only five feet but I sat on my arm. It broke such way as to give me a second wrist. The doctors set it not quite right and I ended up with a weak right wrist. That weak right wrist was key to what happened to me in "Basic" Training. My right wrist simply would not hold me. So I fell thirty six feet off the cargo net.

Trauma at Fourteen

On more clue to my life story: When I was 14 years old, classmates from Junior High cornered me as I walked home from school. They swarmed and sexually molested me. I told nobody at the time. But for years, I had all symptoms of Post Traumatic Stress Syndrome. Five years later I would drop a hint to a sister. Over a decade later, I found myself in the well of a courtroom. I had jury duty and had to explain why I couldn't judge a sexual molestation case. I am still dealing with the aftermath of that incident fifty years later.

12

In Basic Training

A Sham PT Test

During my "Basic" training I had a problem with the overhead bars. Thirty-four rungs were required for the PT Test. Perhaps due to my arm, which had been broken and not re-set properly, perhaps due to the weight I was carrying or because I was frozen with fear at falling, I simply couldn't do the bars. I tried at every meal but no dice.

By the time I was re-cycled and given a choice to go home and I picked the option of staying. It was oblivious I wanted to make it work. Given my educational level, (I had a four year college degree.), my GT score (which shows an IQ of 164), the Army wanted me. But what was to be done?

That's where the "Sham PT Test" came in. My "Drill" sergeant came up with the idea. Someone my size would wear my uniform on the day of the make-up PT test. We would switch identities. I liked the idea. I gave my "Drill" sergeant a bottle of "Beef Eater" gin for his scheme.

13

On Post

Driving Officers

ONE OF MY DUTIES I didn't like was driving officers. They get me to another post where I'd have to buy lunch at my own expense. Once I was promoted to E5, privates and Specialist Four were supposed to perform the driving details. I was kept on the list, but I strove to get off.

The key was to feign a total lack of ability. One morning as I was saluting a Catholic major, I asked him if he had his "O.D." rosary beads. "With my driving You'll need them," I said. I than ran a red light and bounced the sedan over a traffic island. They didn't call on me much to drive after that.

A Story from Vietnam

I served after the Vietnam conflict and before Desert Storm. So I was spared the stresses of combat. But before you read my next section entitled, "I'm Going to Shoot That S.O.B." I want to talk about combat stress and impulse control.

It is true that members of our armed forces face temptations. My story, "I'm Going to Shoot That S.O.B." is about my feelings about an officer I worked with. But feelings are one thing and actions are another. Almost always the troops control their impulses. Only when someone's arrogant and foolish actions are getting people killed do the troops commonly act in order to survive.

A story I heard from a Vietnam combat veteran, illustrates this point. He was the lead man, (walked point) in a "Seek and Destroy" patrol in the jungle. He stopped the patrol because he sensed an ambush ahead. A, "Green," 2nd Lieutenant, "A Butter Bar," ordered the men forward without calling in an air strike first. The teller of the story would no longer volunteer to "Walk point" that is to go first. There was an ambush and the lead soldier was killed. That night they lobbed a grenade into the Lieutenant's tent but they left the pin in. The men were not punished. The Lieutenant was relieved. The command structure recognized that sometimes it's, "Kill or be killed"

I'm Going to Shoot That SOB

"Mein bier, dein bier, unser bier, Moninger Bier!"

When I was stationed in Germany, I drank too much "Moninger Bier" My barracks buddy and I would walk three to four kilometers to go to the "Bistro." There we ate pizza cooked by a Polish man brought to the table by "Moinica," a fetching fraulien. We would share the joint with French Soldiers attracted by the French owner. There we would drink Moninger Bier in steins and glass boots.

The glass boots were part of a drinking game. Participants would take the glass boot, drink as much they dared, set the boot down, hit the table, slap the side of the boot and pass it on. If the boot wasn't knocked onto the floor by a drinking fool or emptied in one swig by someone trying to prove something, the game went on.

Another drinking game was seven, fourteen and twenty-one. The bar-owner would start this game. It was played with dice. A match on the dice's face meant whoever holding them would

On Post

keep them. Otherwise the dice were passed on to the next person. When the cumulative total reached or passed seven, whoever was holding the dice would order a drink. When the cumulative total reached fourteen, whoever was holding the dice would drink the drink. When the cumulative total reached twenty-one whoever was holding the dice would pay for the drink. The result people would order nasty and expensive drinks because someone else might have to drink and or pay for the drinks. It's a good way to get roaring drunk.

One of the reasons we might was want to get drunk were the officers we had to deal with. The most colorful example of those was Captain Dowty, whom we dubbed "Howdy Dowty."

Captain Dowty was a "West Point" graduate with a social climbing wife. He was quite bright but had neither social graces or "Common" Sense. He had been selected for the academy out of some back-woods congressional district. His wife had gotten outa "Oakie-ville" but not advanced much further. The reason was the way Captain Dowty conducted himself.

He went to pick up his wife's relatives at the "Bahnhof," (aka: local train station). He was driving a VW bug. He attempted a left turn cutting off a "Strassenbahn" (aka; street-car). (German Streetcars don't stop for "Autos, "Rubber" wheeled transportation they don't respect).

The result was Captain Dowty's VW bug got crushed into the side of a 2.5 x 120 meter urban train. His brother-in-law left his teeth on the handle over the "Bug's" glove box. The StrassenBahn's conductor got out and cleaned the VW's paint off the streetcar. The bug was totaled. The paint on the StrassenBahn was not even scratched. Captain Dowty was lucky the Strassenbahn didn't run into the "Bug." The streetcar's coupler would've cut the bug in half.

But that was not the only bone-headed maneuver, "Howdy Dowty" pulled. As Headquartors' Design officer, he recommended changes to a heliport which would've made it malfunction. After that he was reassignned.

I worked directly for Howdy Dowty. I remember going to an army dentist during his tenure. The dentist upon discovering I was grinding my teeth down asked me if I was married. I said, "No Sir, that's from saying, 'Yes Sir', to idiots, Sir."

But Howdy Dowty was not the most irksome officer I worked with. That would be Captain C. I had a personality conflict with Captain C. Not that he was a "Bad" Engineer, he reeked of arogance. He reviewed a project of mine and caught every misplaced comma, but missed the fact that if had been bulit as designed that it might collapsed under the weight of troops when they sat on its beachers. Every time he spoke, it was like chalk going the wrong way on a blackboard. But I kept it to myself, and parroted. "Yes Sir."

Then he made me his armed guard for payroll duty. The night before I lie awake thinking, "I'm going to shoot that S. O. B." When I drew my M16 and three rounds, I was a worn out mess. When I reported to "Guard" Captain C, I had other thoughts. As we completed our duty and we were walking the money back to the Finance company I found myself aiming my rifle into the small of Captain C's back thinking, "I'm going to shoot that S. O. B."

F, F and F Yourself

When you know another language vaguely, sometimes the meaning of its slang combines in odd ways with one's native tongue. This is certainly true of Americans' barracks German and English. I remember a quiz show on Armed forces Radio. They were trying to give away some prize. They had a German wife, of an American First Sergeant among the grunts (Infantry), on the phone. They asked for the common name of Sodium Nitrate which of course is salt. (Before we go further you should know that in German slang eggs equal balls.) The sergeant's "Frau" didn't get the clue. So they gave her another one. "What does your husband put on his eggs in the morning?" With no sense of irony, the Frau answered, "Baby powder." The sergeant had a hard time living that one down.

On Post

There's a similar odd twist of meaning between three German verbs and one of the most infamous word in English. "Verstecken, Verbergen and Vonfahren," all start with the "F" sound. Together they are slang for a coping strategy in the German Army. When someone wants you to do something risky or unpleasant you first hide "Verstecken" or have a low profile. If that doesn't work you, "Verbergen," fake out others that you are already busy. If that doesn't work you, you "Vonfahren" you take off or disappear. By sound, it's, "F, F and F Yourself!" And course in English, "F it" or "F yourself" are common expressions in the U.S Army.

The most common, besides "F'ing this and F'ing that," expression is "FTA."or F' the Army. It was against regulations to use either the phrase or the letters while I served. But enforcing that regulation was near impossible.

As a pastor's son, I found "F'ing this and F'ing that" offensive. I told the other soldiers that, "If everything 'F'ed' the army won't have to buy anything. Wall-lockers, Jeeps and rifles would all reproduce." They looked at me like I was nuts. In spite of my feelings I did once get mad enough to use the, "F-Word."

It was time for "Motor Pool" a monthly event where troops maintain assigned vehicles. Mine was a green pick-up truck. The "'Buck' sergeant," in charge of the detail, disappeared into the snack-bar. As each of us finished washing and checking the fluid levels on we were going to lunch without the blessing of the sergeant in charge. I was the only one left when he came out. And I was two hundred meters away towards the mess-hall when he started yelling. He pointed at the ground where I should come as if calling a dog.

I blew up and started yelling, "F' yourself," in the middle of the street, at the top of my lungs.

Thanks: Giving and Receiving Gratitude for America's Troops

Flight of the Frog

"Ribbit, Ribbit"

I approached this little frog (see vase above) and spoke to it. "Ribbit, Ribbit"

It was stting on a shelf in the local Kaufhaus, (A Department Store) in Karlsruhe, West Germany. It was 1979, the second year of my US Army tour in that city. My problem was: I was madly in love with a German girl in another city. (This girl looks a little like the girl I would marry, my beloved wife.) I had met this German girl ten years before in California where her father was taking flight training for Luftansia. I had rekindled the relationship but it wasn't going well. I was desperate so I decided to transform myself into a frog.

At first I planned a frog-mobile; Something I'd sit inside of which would fly through the air hopping. Problem was once it left the ground, I couldn't figure out how to control; where it would land. Since I planned to do this in front of Fraulein's second grade class, I could not be sure I wouldn't crush der kinder in their school yard. That'd be bad for German-American relations.

So I decided to dress as a frog. And so I did: I made a egg-shaped body of canvas. Its belly was made of lime green crepe paper. On the back was dark green paper soaked in glue so it glistened. Atop this was the elpizod head. Incorporated atop that were eyes made of white styrafoam. Below them was the open mouth through which I looked out. The mouth was an inverted V of streched red nylon netting. At the point of the V, I placed one of those things you blow in on new year's eve. Rolled on it was a red tongue. Thus I, as a frog, could kiss back if anyone kissed me. Crowning the frog head was a prince's emlem.

Under this I wore my army issue long johns which I dyed green. On my hands were green army glove linners. On my feet were slip-on shoes covered with green web-feet

But I wasn't going to become just a common frog but a frog-prince. Based on the story where an ugly frog asks a lady to kisss him and becomes a prince. I plotted, "Kiss me I'll become a man and your lover!"

For under the frog uniform was princely attire. I modifed a Superman outfit by keeping the cape and adding a ruffled shirt front. Around my loins, I had golden puffy pants. My webbed feet slipped off to reveal white slippers with gold buckles. Once I took my frog shell off my shoulders, I would grab and don a red felt hat with a yellow feather boa.

It didn't work out well. The first thing that happened: I got arrested.

It was early evening but dark. I finished my outer costume. I started out towards the laundry. There was a wife of one of guys, who was going to teach me how say in German, "Kiss me . . ."

But I forgot to take my I.D. with me. Moving in and out the shadows I scared a jogger. He called the MPs, saying , "I don't what it is, but there's something weird out there." The MPs pulled up in a van. One said, "What's going on?"

The other demanded, "Was ist passeirt?" (German for "What's going on?") I guess they thought I might a terrorist sneaking on post.

So I took off my frog suit. Now, I'm standing in my long johns which I have dyed green. I have no pockets and no I.D. So the MPs took me to their station. There, thankfully, was a MP who went to the same messhall as myself, he vouched for me. But the NCO on duty, an old sergeant, rocked back and forth in a desk chair chanting, "The army ain't what it used to be."

The second thing that happened was I didn't make the impression I wanted. After riding on a train, a bus and two streetcars to arrive to do my thing, I was told I made a better frog than prince. So much for becoming her "Man" and lover.

The third thing was I got my company commander in trouble. It was the annual inspection. The kind where everything is done just so, down to making little hats outa the GIs' socks and rolling your underwear. There a lot of tension in the air. Commanders are afriad their troops will make them look bad.

And my frog unifrom is hanging beside me as I stand for inspection. The inspector got in my face and demanded, "What's this, Specialist Welty!"

"That's my frog uniform. Sir! Class F!" I barked looking straight ahead,

The inspector didn't know what to do. Neither did my commander.

The fourth thing that happened involved miscommunication. I sent two dozen red roses to my intended lover. I sent them with a card it signed, "Ribbit, Ribbit" A drunk delivered the flowers. Also, my intended didn't know who sent the flowers. "German toads go, "Qwak, Qwak!"

The fifth thing that happened didn't actually involve my frog uniform. But I did don a glistening outer coat and fly after this fraulein in our non-affair.

I had worked on a project on the weekend. So I was given my choice of a day off. My fraulein and I planned to get together. She agreed to take the train from Weisbaden a city 130 kilometers away. The journey would take over an hour. We planned to meet at the train station.

I was determined to keep that appointment come hell or high water. The only problem was I was told if our unit went on alert, my day off would be canceled. The night before my big date the rumor-mill started talking about an alert.

At 05:30 the alert was called. I found myself alone in a two man room. My room-mate, a surveyer, was elsewhere on temporary duty. So I decided to stay in my room and sneak out the window at an opportune moment.

My squad leader heard about what I might be trying. (After all my fraulein had sent me flowers for me at our unit.) He came into the hall outside my locked door. He demanded I come out. I thought, he isn't going to get the pass-key. He thinks I wouldn't dare defy him. After awhile he did give up.

I waited until I could see the convoy had formed up two hundred meters away. It was hard to see. It was pouring down rain. Then I put on my grey-white raincoat. I hopped out the window which was ten feet off the ground. I landed in a squat and I ran over to my bike. I unlocked my green touring bike from the fence. I hopped and pedaled like crazy.

People saw me and asked me about it, But I said, "Who me? What are you talking about?" The unit had made their "Soldier of the Month." I couldn't be a liar.

I have done some crazy things for love. I have dressed as a frog. I have been arrested as a frog. I have suffered from disrespect and miscomunication as a frog. I have hopped away like a frog. Let this frog-man tell you after a while it's best to try a new theme and a new girl.

14

As a Veteran

Black Master Sergeant

I encountered "Master Sergeant Mc..." outside the cafeteria. He looked just as I had in uniform with some variations. First: he was two-thirds my size, second he wore a black beret, third he himself was very black and finally and most strangely he wore both Air Force Master Stripes and US Army on his Chest. So I addressed him (*MS = Master Sergeant / RW = Rev. Welty*):

> RW: (*Calmly and politely*) Good Morning Master Sergeant Mc...
>
> MS: (*Somewhat incredulously*) Good morning, Sir!
>
> RW: (*Thinking: Oh well, I just got promoted but I've earned it*) Thank you for your service. Where did you serve?
>
> MS: (*With pride*) Vietnam three tours!
>
> RW: (*Calmly*) Thank you for your service; in what branch did you serve?
>
> (*The Master Sergeant's confused*)
>
> I notice your are wearing Air Force stripes and Army...
>
> MS: (*In short choppy sentences*) I served in the Army, Navy, and I'm US Army Retired!

As a Veteran

(*He shows me three letters he's added to US ARMY—"RET"*)

RW: (*I had not noticed, but I was not surprised, so I calmly said*) So, I see . . .

MS: (*Desperately wanting to be understood*) And I'm 100 percent disabled—mental and physical!

RW: See you in Building 8 (*Mental Health Facility*)

Later we had a conversation inside the cafeteria where he told me that Mc means he's Irish and Mac is Scottish. Weird, but nice fellow and a fellow CalVet.

Talking to Other Vets

You Didn't Know You Were an IED

During a conversation between myself and my wife in a waiting room at the Veterans' Administration's Medical Center a fellow veteran reacted:

Edgar: (*Summing up day*) I'm doing pretty well except I need to lose weight to don my Kilt

Vet: (*Laughs*)

Edgar: (*This is real*) Yeah my wife is wearing the pin for my kilt

(*Turning to Wife*) Amy, my pin you're wearing is a Claymore sword. The army named a landmine as a Claymore.

(*Amy looks bemused*)

Vet: (*To Amy*) You didn't know you were an IED (*Improvised Explosive Device*).

Faulty Vessel

When I came to the VA as a patitent, the chaplains' office was short-staffed. Of three protestants, one had retired, another had been called into active duty. So I volunteered twenty hours a week to help out.

But there was a question of whether my experience fullfilled the requirements for a paid position. But It was judged that I was an untested or faulty vessel unquallified to take a regular staff job.

Hazards of Wearing a Cross

Recently I was wearing a cross at the VA as I often do. A handicapped veteran asked me if I was a chaplain while I was waiting for my meds. I told him no but I voluteered for them. I then ended up being locked into an argument about "Evil" plots by an insane veteran.

PART FOUR

A Pastor's Reflections

15

On Method

Introduction-Theological Reflection

BEFORE WE GET STARTED on my "Pastor's Reflections," let's talk about my method, first is "*Theological Reflection,*" which I'll expand on in the paragraphs below. In my next section I'll descrbe my call to ministry. After that I will describe my *Images of Theology.* Finally I will lay out my process of *Biblical Interpretation*

The book, which is the blueprint for my method, is, Killen, Patricia O'Connell's & DeBeer's, John, *The Art of Theological Reflection.*

The way this book teaches theological reflection in the Christian tradition is my key the writing of the last section of my book, "A Pastor's reflections"

The book taught me a way to be faithful. It has shown me the pitfall of the standpoints of "Certitude" and "Self-Assurance." This book has shown me the way the standpoint of "Exploration" leads to insights, which can result in trans-formative action.

Killen and DeBeer's Book's, "Movement Toward Insight" has taught me about the value of feelings and images as a way towards insight and action. I also like how they have grounded theology in human reflection. Their way of relating tradition, culture, action and/or positions provides a formula for their process.

Thanks: Giving and Receiving Gratitude for America's Troops

The Rose-My Call

The sound of the phone ringing over the Law Students' conversations was unwelcome. My job of managing the school's bookstore during rush was hard enough without interruptions. I looked over as Latoya, my assistant, picked up the receiver with one hand while the fingers of her other hand continued to dance over the cash register keys.

It was Larry I expected on the phone. Thank God for Larry. Although Mr. Stewart often end-ran his efforts, Larry tried to be a fair arbitrator in company politics. He was also there for me when I needed him. Once at the peak of another "Book Rush," I had to call Larry with the news that my Father had had a heart attack. Larry dropped everything, took over my store so I could go to Dad's deathbed. Larry even did international folk dancing, which I enjoyed.

Latoya caught my eye and called out, "Mr. Stewart's on the line."

Great! What would be the disruption from Stewart? Leaving my workstation, I marched towards the phone with a sense of dread. But surely Larry would get him off my back.

A line of impatient future lawyers glared as I edged my way through the mob. Several wanted information, which I provided as I walked. (Being in demand during rush was typical. Once during rush a student followed me into the Men's Room. While I sat on my toilet, a voice from outside of my booth suddenly asked which outline was best for Lowenthal's Con Law.)

I continued answering as I squeezed myself along behind the front counter. Latoya rang up books as fast as a temp could flash the covers towards her. She had cranked out receipts before everything was in bags. Another temp collected signatures on credit card slips. Stepping over stacks of purchases lined up on the floor, I wedged myself into the corner by the phone.

Mr. Stewart asked, "Are you sitting down?"

What, are you nuts? Haven't you ever bothered to come out to our stores during book rush? Where would I put a chair? I sighed

On Method

inwardly, propped myself against the glass enclosed cabinet where we kept the "Class Ring" samples and said, "Yes."

Mr. Stewart intoned, "Larry has been shot and killed in his home."

I replaced the receiver. I walked back in a daze. I came back to my workstation with my head in my hands. I said, more to myself, than the student in front of me, "That's odd, Larry, my friend and boss has been shot and killed."

The student awkwardly muttered, "I'm sorry."

I snapped myself back into the work mode with, "Take this refund slip, fill out the information on the bottom and you can either receive cash at either cash register or make a purchase."

Details came in during the day, bizarre details. It seemed Larry's folk-dancing world was quite different than the one I'd known in San Diego. There Mom and I danced in City parks' buildings with only water or soft drinks. Among Larry's crowd, folk dancing was done in private clubs where liquor was served and drugs were used.

Larry and his dancing friends were involved in other more dangerous activities. One of these was Russian roulette. The news I was being forced to accept was that Larry, who I had relied on for good sense, was not only dead but had killed himself.

Larry, my "Rational, reliable" boss, who I'd thought I knew as a friend, had gotten high in his home, put a revolver to his head and blew his brains out of his skull. And this madness happened, in the context of folk dancing, which I'd known as wholesome.

During the rest of that long day, Latoya quietly did her job but also served as my sounding board. She grew concerned as each new detail of the news bewildered me. Finally in a lull in the afternoon, she offered to close up so I could leave. For once, I agreed.

I showed Latoya how I wanted the checks, credit card slips and cash bundled and placed in the safe. I'd have to come in early the next day. Hopefully I could get to the bank. Reconciling receipts and making reports would have to wait.

It was risky. Management preferred that daily receipts (which in that time of year totaled in the tens of thousands of dollars) be taken each night to the bank's night drop. (My predecessor had been fired for delaying deposits.) And, I couldn't afford to fall behind during those twelve-hour days.

But I needed to be away. I prayed in the morning, I could get to the bank. I prayed no undecipherable problems would prevent me from having my manager's reports ready for the next day's noontime courier. Then I left for church.

United University Church

I had planned as I always did during "Book Rush" to arrive half way through the Bible study group I co-led at United University Church. But arriving early would give me time to myself, time to pray, and time to ask God for guidance.

As I approached our sanctuary's Italian Romanesque façade, I noted the Hebrew figures in the bas-relief. David stroked his harp. Abraham held the dagger and flaming cauldron of sacrifice. Moses grasped the scroll of "Torah." Elijah clasped the prophetic mantle. I walked into the cloister. Two kneeling angels faced each other where the body of Jesus had lain in his tomb above me as I opened the chapel door.

On Method

The cool interior was lit only by the glow of pastel stained glass. Filtered afternoon light reflected off cream-colored textured stucco walls. I settled into a pale oak pew. Then I saw it. On the altar was a single rose in a crystal glass vase. I hurried towards the office and caught our Church Secretary on her way out.

She explained that the mother of a twenty-year-old student had placed the rose. Her daughter had been a member of USC's marching band. An auto accident had suddenly ended her life. Her memorial had been held that day.

I returned to my pew. I turned around and looked through the open doors of the narthex. There I contemplated one of our few stained glass picture windows. Santa Barbara, the patron saint of architects and victims of sudden death, stared back at me.

I remembered that the window was dedicated to the architect's daughter, killed at twenty in an auto accident. She, too, had been a member of USC's marching band. She had died over fifty years earlier. Such similar tragedies spanning so many years.

I sat in the sacred space of our sanctuary. Although still bewildered by the sudden news of Larry's senseless death, I felt comforted. I was where others had come in confusion. I could feel there was a real need for people to feel God's presence, especially at intense periods in their lives. I realized that faith communities endure as anchors in the uncertain flow of human life.

On Method

I felt enveloped by the Church and called to serve. Soon I would become a lay speaker and preach. Next, I would offer the role of God's representative to the dying and bereaved. Then after seminary, I would don the stole of a pastor and offer believers the presence of God in Word and Sacrament.

My "Call" had started with the ring of a telephone across a crowded room. And now it lasted my whole life. Let it always be so.

Images of Theology

A Graphic Exploration of the Trinity: A Set of Images Based on Triangles and the Color Wheel

As a draftsman and a pastor's son, I sat down at my drawing board during my time in the army to explore my beliefs. The following drawings and descriptions are the result.

God of Light vs. the Darkness

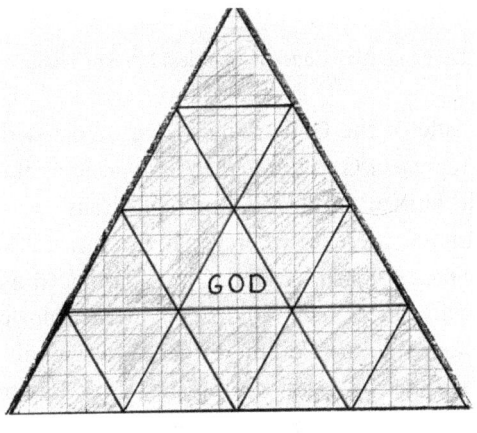

Good and Evil

With a 30/60 triangle I drew an equal sided triangle to represent God and colored it white to represent the source of all light and goodness. Around it I drew other triangles to represent partial truths about God. Around all of the triangles I drew a border of black to represent the absence of light or good, this represents evil, which is overcome by the light of God.

God in Three Persons

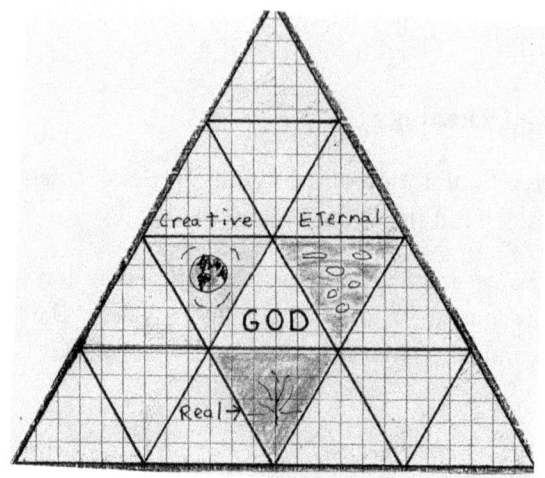

A Core Christian Concept, The Next Level of Triangle

Off of each side of the God triangle, I constructed three more triangles to represent God the *Father/Creator*, Jesus the *Son*/God made *Real* in human terms and God's and Jesus' agent the *Holy Spirit, a Sustaining* presence wherever and whenever two or three gather in the name of Jesus or God. Our Christian triune I further represented with the primary colors. Yellow the color of dawn of creation I assigned to the God the Father. As a symbol of creation I have depicted the cooling gases of planet earth. Red the color of the fire in which God became real to Moses Note: The bush which is not consumed and of the red of Christ's blood and communion wine or juice, I assigned to our Savior/Jesus, the Son of God. Blue the color of the sky, the air in which the Spirit blows, I assigned to the Holy Spirit.

On Method

Partial Summaries of God

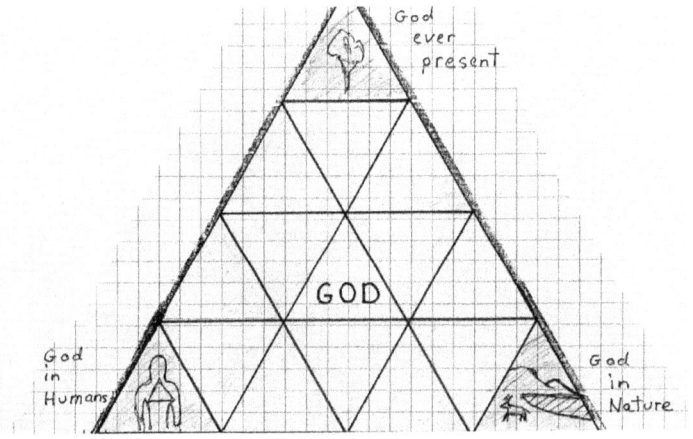

The Gray Triangles

On the tips of the outermost triangle surrounding the White God triangle I have placed gray triangles. Each represents partial summaries of God's nature which overall is beyond human knowing. On top of this greater triangle is *God Ever-Present* with a mirror representing how human see themselves in *present* time according to *1 Corinthians 12:13a KJV* "In a glass/mirror darkly/not clearly." If you think this is absolutely true, answer the questions of Job or Jesus when he cried out from the cross, "My God, my God, why have you forsaken me?" *Matthew 27:46b NRSV*. The Grey triangle to the bottom left represents *God Within Human Effort*. To believe that is the whole truth about God is to worship humanity instead of the divine. The bottom right gray triangle depicts *God in Nature*. Of course, God transcends the creation.

Thanks: Giving and Receiving Gratitude for America's Troops

The Wheel of Life

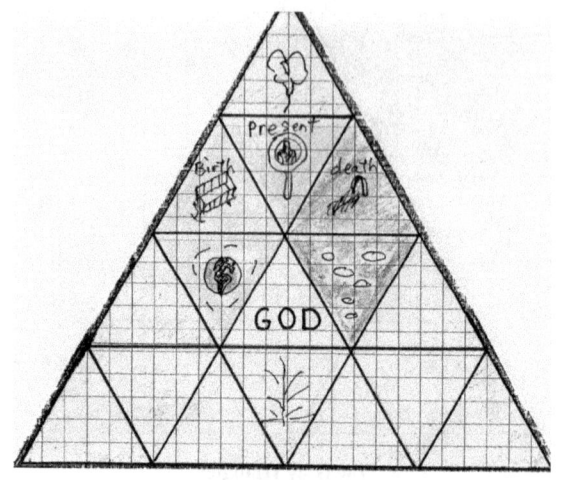

God Ever-Present in Our Life Cycle

Adjacent to the triangle of God as *Father/Creator*, I constructed a yellow green triangle representing human *birth*. Next I drew a triangle in green with a lily referring to Jesus' words, "Consider the lilies, how they grow: they neither toil or spin; yet I tell even Solomon in all his glory was not clothed like one of these. But if God so clothes the grass of the field, which is alive today and tomorrow is thrown into the oven, how much more will he clothe you-you of little faith." *Luke 12:27-28 NRSV* (Note: This is next to a gray triangle with a mirror in which is the refection of a human being.) Next to it I drew a blue/green triangle representing the fate of all flesh, which is the grave or *death*. Note this connects to God's *Eternal Spirit*.

On Method

Human Creativity

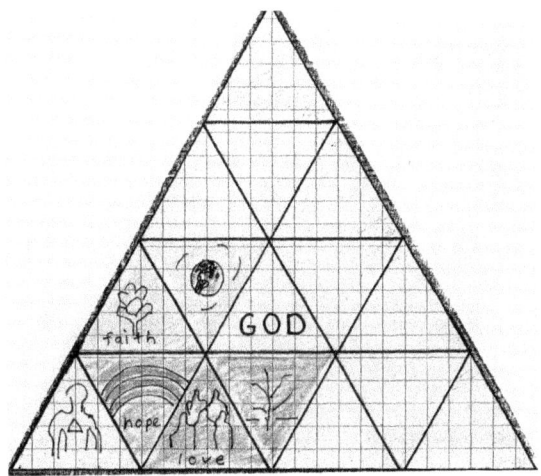

God Within Human Effort

On the other side of the triangle of God as *Father/Creator*, I constructed a mustard colored triangle representing *faith*. Note the words of Jesus; "For truly, I tell you, if you have *faith* the size of a *mustard* seed, you will say to this mountain, 'Move from here to there,' and it will move; and nothing will be impossible for you." *Matthew 17:20 NRSV* An orange colored triangle I picked to represent God's *hope* for humankind which is also represented by the rainbow God formed in the sky after the flood of the Noah story. Red/orange forms the background of a symbol of all kinds of humans, which mandates the need for brotherly/sisterly *love*. These concepts come from scripture: *1 Corinthians 13:13 NRSV* reads "And now *faith*, *hope*, and *love* abide, these three: and the greatest of these is *love*." Note all of this connects to God as *Savior/ Jesus Christ*.

Thanks: Giving and Receiving Gratitude for America's Troops

Slices of Reality

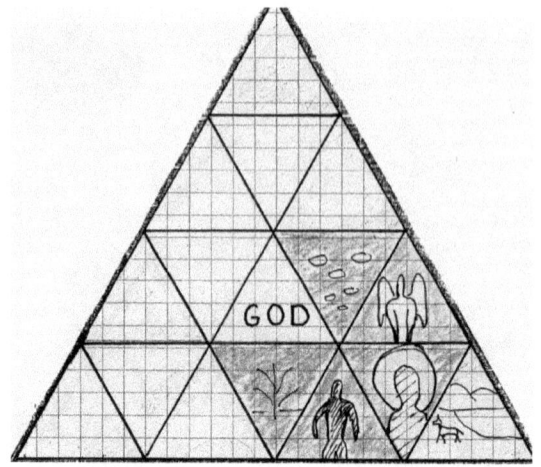

God in Nature; Human Bodies, Minds and Spirits

Adjacent to the triangle of God as *Savior/Jesus Christ*, I have constructed a red/purple colored triangle representing our *bodies*. Next to that I placed a purple triangle, which has a head with a creative/yellow halo representing our *minds*. A blue/purple background highlights a winged figure representing our spirits. Note this connects to God's *Eternal Spirit*.

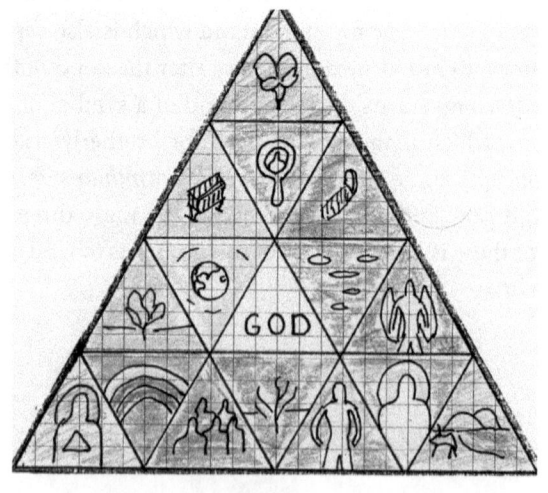

A Complex God

On Method

Thus we have a mature, or a complex and serious spiritual System. We read in I Corinthians 13:9-12 KJV; "For we know in part, and we prophesy in part. But when that which is perfect is come, then that which is in part shall be done away. When I was a child, I spake as a child, I understood as a child, I thought as a child; but when I became a man I put away childish things. For now we see through a glass darkly; but then face to face: now I know in part; but I will know even as I am known."

Too many theologies are childish. *Images in Theology* is an attempt to look at the bigger more complete picture. Some want to put Jesus in their hip pocket, a presence that'll get one home when they are rip roaring drunk. Others think nature is all God is. Still others see God within themselves to the point of self-worship. *Images of Theology* is more complete, but is still not the "Whole 'Truth.'"

Biblical Interpretation

My approach to biblical interpretation is shaped by my experience. I have read through the entire Bible two to three times as a result of a year long reading plan. For years I co-led a bible study group as an Elder in the Presbyterian Church (USA) and as a United Methodist Lay Speaker. Our studies were based on the Revised Common Lectionary. So was my preaching when, after earning a four year Masters of Divinity Degree, I was ordained as a Minister of Word and Sacrament to serve a United Church of Christ Church in Rochester, New York. Thereafter, I also provided pulpit supply for two Lutheran (ELCA) congregations. The first was for two to three months in a small village in upstate New York. The second was for almost five years in Tiburon, California.

To prepare for "Bible Study" and preaching, I used annotated Bibles, Bible dictionaraes and commentaries. The best annotated Bible I've found is the *New Oxford Annotated Bible*. I like the *Anchor Bible Dictionary* in six volumes. Commentaraes I've used include the *Interpreter's Bible* in twelve volumes and its new edition. I also use *Mastering the New Testament* in twelve volumes and

Thanks: Giving and Receiving Gratitude for America's Troops

Mastering the Old Testament in twenty volumes. Preaching guides include the *New Procalmation, Preaching the Revised Common Lectionary and Preaching Through the Christian Year.*

16

Issues

Communism: What and Why **by Edgar Shirley Welty, Sr.**

Entered into the US, Congressional Record by Representative Bob Wilson of San Diego California, August 10, 1954

Rev. Edgar Shirley Welty, Sr., Photo by Margo (Ruth) Butner

Thanks: Giving and Receiving Gratitude for America's Troops

Communism or socialism could be defined as the rough road back to barbarism mistakenly labeled a short cut to destiny.

Many years ago students of government noticed that the development of government theory and institution developed in cycles that swung first towards the liberal and then toward the reactionary in general feeling. It was also noticed that over a period of time the general movement was towards a liberal direction.

Now in the early nineteenth century (150 to 100 years ago) the greater part of Europe and the world was still dominated by the ideas of society inherited from feudal times and even in the infant Republic of the United States practices now seen as an important part of democracy would have been regarded as unthinkable anarchy.

Everywhere workmen labored 12 to 14 hours a day 7 days a week. Everywhere education was limited and children worked long hours for little more than enough for poor food to keep from starving. Nowhere could women vote or even control their own property and most of the nations of the world still condoned slavery.

In England, in France, and in America, politicians, patriots and philosophers had begun the movement toward human freedom and individual rights, and from these centers the challenge of mankind's dreams and hopes rang out through all the world.

In Germany, where feudal serfdom still existed alongside a growing learning and beginning of industry, a young man of a wealthy family studied philosophy. He had no personal religion and he was of a bitter and frustrated disposition, unsuccessful at love, and unacceptable as a teacher, he blamed everyone but himself. Gradually he became associated with the most radical elements, and, supported by the wealthy father of a friend, this human failure poured the gall of his frustation and bitterness into a series of distorted writings that have been unparaelled in the havoc they have caused.

This was Karl Marx, the father of communism and socialism. (My father, like so many others, wrongly paints with the same brush, "Socialism," "Communism" and "Marxism.")

Issues

It was his contention that society was moving to the left anyway, then the sensible thing to do was seize power by force and bring about the ultimate changes quickly under a temporary dictatorship.

Like many others, he let his personal defects and hates influence his thinking. So history as he saw it would wipe out the wealthy and aristocractic classes that had rejected him and the laborers would be the army that would do it. He hungered and thristed for vengeance and could not wait to see bloody heads roll as they had a few years earlier in France.

So he proposed a dictatorship to hurry the work of a world revoulution. Marx was both a poor student of history and philosophy. He completely failed to realize that a bad means cannot produce a good end.

But he wrote so cleverly and so convincingly that his writing have been the chief tool of professional rabble rousers and demagogs ever since his time.

Now, in our own day, the foolishness of his theories have become apparent, for the whole world is divided into two camps. At the head of one camp is the Soviet Union (Russia) and at the head of the other is our own country.

The Soviet Union is the product of communist revolution and 35 years of communist dictatorship.

Instead of withering away, instead of providing the self-government, peace and plenty for a happy people, the Soviet Union has fastened a growing tyranny upon the people of Russia. It has delibratly slaughterd, starved, and imprisoned millions of its own people in order to impose its rule. It has produced poverty and fear for its own people, while it has used its resources to invade and enslave the weaker nations on its borders. From day to day it punges onward in fear and desperation, imperiling the whole world.

In the meantime our own country has led the world in a steady evolution that has produced the highest standard of living the world has ever known.

Here any man with normal intelligence and temperate habits can live a life such as the wealthest nobles could not have lived a hundred years ago.

Almost every man owns some part of our industrial system through an insurance policy if nothing else. Millions own their own homes, farms and businesses. Thousands own bonds, have money in the bank, or own at least a few shares in some company. Living conditions and the rights of labor have improved beyond the wildest dreams of even 50 years ago. Every child can get a fine education. The aged, the orphaned the underprivleged can turn to any one of many agenices for help yet all of this has come quietly, with no civil war, no blood purges, no famine, and no real suffering.

America is far from perfect; a hundred years from now our grandchildren's grandchildren will still find much to do to improve the best we can bequeath them, yet we should have confidence to work steadily ahead, for the furture belongs to the free.

Surely a tree shall be known by its fruit and the good tree that bears good fruit will be tended and treasured, but the poor tree that bears bad fruit shall be cut down and burned.

Moral Injury: A Muddled Concept

As we explore ways to thank active duty military and veterans the issue of *moral injury* comes up. Because it is so new a concept it is still muddled. Note: The following quotes from the article Maguen and Litz listed among the *Resources* of this book shows the tentative nature of *moral injury*.

Definition: "An Act (by a member of the military or those around him or her) of serious transgression that leads to serious inner conflict because the experience is at odds with core ethical and moral beliefs is called *moral injury*."

"War zone events which may contribute to moral injury: *Betrayal* (e.g.. leadership failures, betrayal by peers, failure to live up to one's own moral standards, betrayal by trusted civilians) *disproportionate violence* (e.g., mistreatment of enemy combatants and acts of revenge), *incidents involving civilians* (e.g. destruction of civilian property and assault) and *within-rank violence* (e.g., military sexual trauma, friendly fire and fragging)

". . . Signs or symptoms of moral injury (are described by Maguen and Litz as): social problems, trust issues, spiritual/existential issues, psychological symptoms and self-deprecation."

". . . Suggestions about ways to repair moral injury; these can be categorized into spiritually directed, socially directed and individually directed interventions."

The "Mainline" Church Jumps the Rails

There is an old term for the major Protestant denominations in America. They are called "Mainline" after the rail line between New York and Philadelphia the old center of life in the US. It is my contention that these denominations have jumped the rails in three ways. First, they got out of step with their congregates by learning but not preaching advanced biblical criticism. (See Jack Good's book *The Dishonest Church,*) Second, mainline seminaries, particularly mine, became havens for "Draft Dodgers" during the Vietnam War. (When the draft ended, half of the students at San Francisco Theological Seminary quit.) Third, the mainline national governing bodies aligned themselves far to the left of their parishioners on issues such as; Women's Issues, Inclusive language, Labor Rights, Liberation Theology and Gay Rights. (See Rogers' book, *Claiming The Center*.) The result has been that mainline churches, once a mainstay of American life have been marginalized. This has happened directly as result of their misalignments. It has happened indirectly through internal divisions within the denominations. (See the Office of the General Assembly of Presbyterian Church (USA), *Is Christ Divided?*).

17

God and America's Early History
The Religious Roots of America and Her Wars

The "Old" World Soil

MOST PEOPLE READING THIS will identify the nation of the United States of America with the term "America". But the name "America" is much older than the U. S. A. That term for all of the lands opened by Spain and Portugal's voyages of discovery was in use centuries before the "Founders" of the United States of America conceived of our new nation. The religious roots of America and her wars are entwined in those centuries. Other soil for these roots involve British political and religious history. Another set of factors is the international relations within Europe at the time.

After Columbus' sailed across the Atlantic in 1492, the pope divided responsibility for "America" between Spain and Portugal. England, which soon there after, declared her religious independence from Rome, was not inclined to accept the pope's decision. English monarchs after Henry the 8th. did not see the pope as the "Vicar of Christ" rather they called him, "The 'Whore' of 'Babylon'" and identified him with "The Anti-Christ"

God and America's Early History

Spain, Portugal and France were England's rival powers in Europe and in the grab for lands in the "New World". The fact is all of these rivals were Catholic while England was protestant. England, especially after Spain attempted to mount an invasion with her "Armada", felt she was being out-flanked. So the English throne took an interest the colonization of America to counter-balance the power of her European rivals.

The other soil for America's religious roots are found deep in British political and religious history. After Henry the 8th. replaced the pope's leadership of the English church with his own, he did not define the nature of the English church. Mary, "Queen of Scots" even tried to reconnect the English Church with Rome. It did not work for most English citizens saw being Catholic as being disloyal to God, their monarch and the English nation. Even if most of the English accepted that their nation should be protestant that did not settle the question of what kind of worship and theology should prevail. The English Civil War may have been provoked by Charles I's personality, but it was largely religious issues, which fueled it.

Whether or not the worship-leader should wear priestly robes and other vestments or an academic robe or no distinctive garb at all, was one hotly debated question. Another issue is whether worship should be an enactment of the sacrifice of God's Son, Jesus Christ with the transubstantiation of the communion wine and bread into the blood and body of Jesus centered around an altar or the "Lord's Supper" memorialized around a table. Should communion be an occasional event with most services centered around the "Word" from the pulpit was also a topic of contention. Lastly was the issue of how much control individuals and congregations should have over their religious life and how much national uniformity should be enforced.

Some issues, which seem to be only political, have religious roots. One question involves the relative power of the British Parliament and her monarch. If England's anointed monarch rules by "Divine Right" why does he or she need the cooperation of the people representative? Answering that question wrong cost Charles I his head!

Since the bulk of settlers which came to the thirteen colonies, which would form the core the United States of America came from the British Isles these issues formed the religious roots of the new republic.

18

Religion at the Time of Our Nation's Birth

THE STATE OF RELIGION, when we in the U. S. A. declared our independence, is clearly described in William Placher's book on his History of Theology. Which relates this situation on page 261.
". . . in 1776, every state except Rhode Island still required some sort of religious affirmation from anyone seeking public office, and Connecticut (until 1818), New Hampshire (Until 1819) and Massachusetts (Until 1833) still recognized an established church with special privileges and tax support. People like Jefferson and Franklin sought to limit the churches' influence on the state, but it was principally the sheer fact of religious diversity, which ruled out an established church on the national level. Congregationalists dominated Massachusetts, Anglicans Virginia, and so on, but no denomination had a dominant position in the whole country. As a result, . . . a least-common denominator Christianity rather like Deism came to characterize public occasions in the United States."

Perhaps the phase which sums this better than any other comes from our Declaration of Independence there Thomas Jefferson speaks of "Nature and nature's God" It is appropriate wording for a man who edited out all of miracles in the New Testament. It is also appropriate wording for a least-common denominator faith behind which the country could unite.

Thanks: Giving and Receiving Gratitude for America's Troops

Our nation's founders had the motto "One of many one". They were keenly aware of the chaos, which came to Europe with the Reformation. Religious wars had torn apart many nations. Many of our earliest leaders were also old enough to remember the English Civil War where Puritan armies fought against Anglican forces. Fresh also were stories of Protestant and Catholic martyrs. Our founders knew they could not hope to fight the British if they did not "Hang together" and religious differences would divide them.

That does not mean there were no sectarian religious motives in the American Revolution. But they operated on a state-by-state basis. Congregationalists in Massachusetts were loyal to "The church without a bishop for the country without a king". In all the state militias, pastors often lead their congregations into battle. Among the troops also were chaplains, which came mostly from the established churches.

19

City on a Hill

Jesus' Original "Word" in his "Sermon on the Mount"

BEFORE READING THIS SECTION it might be worthwhile to the reader to go over my *Personal Expanded Paraphase of Matthew 4:25–5:1–2, 12–17.* "A City on a Hill" in Context in the appendix of this book.

San Francisco: "A City on Some Hills"
If you know where to look, you can make out the buildings of "The City" over 20 miles away. This picture is taken from a "Mount" or hill near my home in Marin County.

I believe Jesus had a similar vantage point when he went up "the Mount."

Thanks: Giving and Receiving Gratitude for America's Troops

Perhaps he pointed out Jerusalem, which by the time this Gospel was published, would be reduced to a shameful ruin for lack of faithfulness. Jesus words would have been heard as a judgment against people could be seen as having lost their favor (purpose) as "Salt of the earth" or placed their lamps "Under the grain measure" rather than "on the lamp-stand," where, "it shines for all who are in the house."

Charity in John Winthrop's "City"

I think John Winthrop words speak for themselves.

> *For we must consider that we shall be as a city upon a hill. The eyes of all people are upon us.* So that if we shall deal falsely with our God in this work we have undertaken, and so cause Him to withdraw His present help from us, we shall be made a story and a by-word through the world.
>
> Thus stands the cause between God and us. We are entered into covenant with Him for this work. We have taken out a commission. The Lord hath given us leave to draw our own articles. We have professed to enterprise these and those accounts, upon these and those ends. We have hereupon besought Him of favor and blessing. Now if the Lord shall please to hear us, and bring us in peace to the place we desire, then hath He ratified this covenant and sealed our commission, and will expect a strict performance of the articles contained in it; but *if we shall neglect the observation* of these articles which are the ends we have propounded, and, dissembling with our God, *shall fall to embrace this present world and prosecute our carnal intentions, seeking great things for ourselves and our posterity,* the Lord will surely break out in wrath against us, and be revenged of such a people, and make us know the price of the breach of such a covenant.
>
> Now the only way to avoid this shipwreck, and to provide for our posterity, is to follow the counsel of Micah, to do justly, to love mercy, to walk humbly with our God. For this end, we must be knit together, in this work,

as one man. We must entertain each other in brotherly affection. *We must be willing to abridge ourselves of our superfluities, for the supply of others' necessities.* We must uphold a familiar commerce together in all meekness, gentleness, patience and liberality.

If our hearts shall turn away, so that we will not obey, but shall be seduced, and worship other Gods, our pleasure and profits, and serve them; it is propounded unto us this day, *we shall surely perish out of the good land whither we pass over this vast sea to possess it.*

*Therefore let us choose life,
that we and our seed may live,
by obeying His voice and cleaving to Him,
For He is our life and our prosperity.*

It has been almost four centuries since these words were spoken aboard the flagship of a fleet of Puritan immigrants. But they are still true in this pastor's mind.

The "City" in Washington's Vision

Our first president offered a lot of advice in his *Farewell Address*. These short selections from those I have reprinted give a hint as to some of our founders' vision of nation or "City" in a larger sense. The features of this vision included among other things governance without party politics. I think Americans could and possibly should seek to reconstruct that founding vision. Read and think!

This government, the offspring of our own choice, uninfluenced and unawed, adopted upon full investigation and mature deliberation, completely free in its principles, in the distribution of its powers, uniting security with energy, and containing within itself a provision for its own amendment, has a just claim to your confidence and your support.

They (party politicians) serve to organize faction, to give it an artificial and extraordinary force; to put, in the place of the delegated will of the nation the will of a party, too often a small but artful and enterprising minority of

> the community; and, according to the alternate triumphs of different parties.
>
> However combinations or associations of the above description may now and then answer popular ends, they are likely, in the course of time and things, to become potent engines, by which cunning, ambitious, and unprincipled men will be enabled to subvert the power of the people and to usurp for themselves the reins of government, destroying afterwards the very engines which have lifted them to unjust dominion.

The "City" Breaks in Two

While all of Lincoln's Address is worthwhile reading, this last part is particularly worth thinking about. For our nation having been broken in two needed healing.

> With malice toward none, with charity for all, with firmness in the right as God gives us to see the right, let us strive on to finish the work we are in, to bind up the nation's wounds, to care for him who shall have borne the battle and for his widow and his orphan, to do all which may achieve and cherish a just and lasting peace among ourselves and with all nations.

John Kennedy Revives the Theme

John Kennedy revived the theme of the "City" as a term for our national effort. Note from the passage below how he admonishs us.

> Today the eyes of all people are truly upon us—and our governments, in every branch, at every level, national, state and local, must be as a city upon a hill — constructed and inhabited by men aware of their great trust and their great responsibilities. For we are setting out upon a voyage in 1961 no less hazardous than that undertaken by the Arbella in 1630. We are committing ourselves to tasks of statecraft no less fantastic than that

of governing the Massachusetts Bay Colony, beset as it was then by terror without and disorder within. History will not judge our endeavors—and a government cannot be selected—merely on the basis of color or creed or even party affiliation.

Ronald Reagan Transforms the "City"

President Reagan said

> I have spoken of the shining city all my political life, but I don't know if I ever quite communicated what I saw when I said it. But in my mind it was a tall proud city built on rocks stronger than oceans, wind-swept, God-blessed, and teeming with people of all kinds living in harmony and peace, a city with free ports that hummed with commerce and creativity, and if there had to be city walls, the walls had doors and the doors were open to anyone with the will and the heart to get here. That's how I saw it and see it still . . .

And I as a pastor want to remnd my fellow Americans, that our nation shines as a "City" only as a reflection of God's divine purpose. Jesus the Christ is the true, "Light of the world." Through the power of the "Holy Spirit," America can only truly "shine" if faithfull to a vision beyond herself.

Obama and Washington

Both Washington and Obama asks us to see beyond political divides. Washington is his *Farewell Address* and Obama in his *Red State, Blue State Speech*. See Appendix.

Conclusion

20

What Would God Have Us Do?

Avoiding Worshiping the "Rate of Return" and Ourselves

ONCE ON MY WAY home from an appointment at the VA, I was running low on gas. But, I had lost my ATM card that morning. I had a personal check from a local bank. It was pouring down rain but nobody would sell me gas. Not even a bank would honor my check. I barely made it to a branch of my bank to get cash and make it home.

Call me foolish but if the gas stations and that bank I went to were more focused on customer service instead of reducing risk and saving costs by not cashing checks, I think we would be better off. I think too many Americans worship their rate of return on investment to the exclusion of all else.

The other blind spot of our citizens seems to be the assumption that America is always right and has the right and even duty impose her will by military means. We are about 5 percent of the world's population. How can we believe in democracy and impose our will on the other 95 percent? And the 1 percent of Americans in the military gets the thankless task of this impossible mission.

21

A Final Word

For Veterans in Particular and The Public in General

THIS BOOK HAS BEEN addressed first to my fellow veterans and our active duty military who will become veterans. After reading it I would hope if any of you are in trouble personally, you will go to the Veterans Administration or your commanders for help. Or to get help online; check out the web sites listed in the *Resources* section of this book. If you are reacting to policy implications of my reflections please work with a veterans organization. And above all accept the thanks of your fellow Americans.

As for the general public: Listen to veterans, support and thank them.

Postscript

Thanking Those who had Served but are Now Passed

A Sacred Honor

I AM A CHAPLAIN with the honorary rank of captain with the United States Volunteers/America. This is a veterans' service organization, which claims the legacy of Teddy Roosevelt's "Rough Riders." We provide "Final Military Honors" at veterans' funerals and committal services at National Cemeteries.

I was recently called by the Commander of California's 31st Regiment to provide services for a "Rosie the Riveter." She had assembled aircraft in World War Two.

I came up with the texts for two services and ran off programs for each. I put on my modified Army Service Uniform aka Dress Blues and got into a rental car. I drove nearly 40 miles to get to the funeral home. There I was met by a crowd of 75 people including uniformed Veterans of Foreign Wars members, who folded the flag off the casket and played. Taps. I, of course, led worship.

After an interval we formed a funeral procession. Veterans on motorcycles with flags provided an escort. We drove over sixty miles to Sacramento Valley National Cemetery.

Thanks: Giving and Receiving Gratitude for America's Troops

Once at the cemetery, there was another interval. As we offered the appropriate prayers, we were accompanied by veterans on horseback with flags.

After I gave my final benediction, I got in my rental car for a long drive home. Along the way I realized what a "Sacred honor" it had been to be the chaplain at these two services.

A Service of Hope in the Resurection for Faye Miller Crete

A "Rosie the Riveter"
She worked in an aircraft factory in WW2
14 Jan 1926—18 Mar 2015
at
San Leandro Funeral Home
March 30, 2015
Chaplain: (Capt.) Edgar S. Welty, Jr. USV-A

Thanking Those who had Served but are Now Passed

Gathering to Hear God's Word

Invocation

Blessed be the God and Father of our Lord Jesus Christ, the source of all mercy and the God of all consolation. He comforts us in all our sorrows with the consolation we ourselves have received from God

Thanks be to God

Scripture Romans 6:3-5

> When we were baptized in Christ Jesus, we were baptized into his death. We were buried therefore with him by baptism into death, so that, as Christ was raised from the dead by the glory of the Father, we too might live a new life. For if we have been united with Christ with a death like his, we certainly will be united with him in a resurrection like his.

Prayer

The Lord be with you
> *And also with you*

Let us pray.
    O God, who gave us birth, you are ever more ready to hear than we are to pray. You know our needs before we ask, and our ignorance in asking. Show us now your grace, that as we face the mystery of death we may see the light of eternity. Speak to us once more your solemn message of life and death. Help us to live as those who are prepared to die, and when our days here are ended, enable us to die as those who go forth to live, so that living or dying, our life may be in Jesus Christ our risen Lord.
    Amen.

Thanks: Giving and Receiving Gratitude for America's Troops

Hearing God's Word

First Lesson Romans 8:38-39

I am convinced that neither death, nor life, nor angels, nor rulers, nor things present, nor things to come, nor powers, nor height, nor depth, nor anything else in all creation, will be able to separate us from the love of God in Christ Jesus our Lord.
Thanks be to God!

Psalm 23 LBW (Read Responsively)
Pastor / *Congregation*

> The LORD is my shepherd; I shall not be in want.
> *He makes me lie down in green pastures; and leads me beside still waters.*
> He revives my soul and guides me along right pathways for his name's sake.
> *Though I walk through the valley of the shadow of death,*
> I shall `fear no evil; for you are with me; your rod and your staff they comfort me.
> *You spread a table before me in the presence of those who trouble me;*
> You have anointed my head with oil; and my cup is running over.
> *Surely your goodness and mercy shall follow me all the days of my life;*
> And I will dwell in the house of the LORD forever.

Gospel as Fulfillment of Ancient Prophecy John 10:14; Isaiah. 40:11

Jesus said: I am the good shepherd. I know my own and my own know me. He will feed his flock like a shepherd; he will gather the lambs in his arms, and carry them in his bosom.
Thanks be to God!

Thanking Those who had Served but are Now Passed

Responding to God's Word

Living together in trust and hope, we confess our faith.
 I believe in God, the Father almighty, creator of heaven and earth.
 I believe in Jesus Christ, God's only Son, our Lord, who was conceived by the Holy Spirit, born of the Virgin Mary, suffered under Pontius Pilate, was crucified, died, and was buried; he descended to the dead. On the third day he rose again; he ascended into heaven, he is seated at the right hand of the Father, and he will come again to judge the living and the dead. I believe in the Holy Spirit, the holy catholic church, the communion of saints, the forgiveness of sins, the resurrection of the body, and the life everlasting. Amen.

Prayers of the People

For our sister Faye, Let us pray to pray to our Lord Jesus Christ who said, "I am the resurrection and the life. Lord, you consoled Martha and Mary in their distress;
 Draw near to us who mourn for Kay, and dry the tears of those who weep.
 Hear us Lord.
 You wept at the grave of Lazarus your friend; comfort us in our sorrow
 Hear us Lord.
 You raised the dead to life; give to our sister eternal life.
 Hear us Lord.
 You promised paradise to the repentant thief; Bring Faye to the joys of heaven
 Hear us Lord.
 Our sister was washed in baptism and anointed with the Holy Spirit; give her fellowship with all your saints.
 Hear us Lord.
 She was nourished at your table on earth; welcome her at your table in the heavenly kingdom
 Hear us Lord.

Comfort us in our sorrows at the death of Faye; let our faith be our consolation and eternal life our hope
Amen.

The Lord's Prayer *KJV* (Please stand.)

Let us pray as Jesus has taught us:
Our Father who art in heaven, hallowed be Thy name, Thy kingdom come,
Thy will be done, on earth as it is in heaven. Give us this day our daily bread,
And forgive us our trespasses as we forgive those who trespass against us:
And lead us not into temptation but deliver us from evil. For Thine is the kingdom, the power, and the glory forever and ever. Amen.

Commendation

Into your hands, O merciful Savior, we commend your servant, Faye Miller Crete. Acknowledge, we humbly beech you, a sheep of your fold, a lamb of your own flock, a sinner of your own redeeming. Receive her into the arms of you mercy, into the blessed rest of everlasting peace, and into the glorious company of the saints in light. *Amen.*

Going Forth in the Hope of God's Word

Charge (Matthew 22:37-40)

Go out into the world in peace
Love the Lord your God
With all your heart, with all your soul, with all your mind.
and love your neighbor as yourself

Thanking Those who had Served but are Now Passed

Blessing (Hebrews 13:20, 21)

The God of peace.
 Who brought back from the dead our Lord Jesus,
 Make you complete in everything good, So that you may do God's will, working among us that which is pleasing in God's sight through Jesus Christ.
 To whom be the glory forever and ever! *Amen*

Commitment Service

At the Sacramento Valley National Cemetary
For Faye Miller Crete

A "Rosie the Riveter"
She worked in an aircraft factory in WW2

14 Jan 1926—18 Mar 2015
Chaplain: (Captain.) Edgar S. Welty, Jr. USV-A

Opening Words

In the midst of life we are in death; of whom may we seek for succor, but of thee, O Lord, who for our sins art justly displeased?

Yet, O Lord God most holy, O Lord most mighty, O holy and merciful Savior, deliver us not into the bitter pangs of eternal death.

Thou knowest, Lord, the secrets of our hearts; shut not thy merciful ears to our prayer; but spare us, Lord most holy, O God most mighty, O holy and merciful Savior, thou most worthy judge eternal. Suffer us not, at our last hour, through any pains of death, to fall from thee

Thanks: Giving and Receiving Gratitude for America's Troops

Commital

In sure and certain hope of the resurrection to eternal life through our Lord Jesus Christ, we commend to Almighty God our sister Faye; and we commit her body to the ground; earth to earth, ashes to ashes, dust to dust. The Lord bless her and kept her, the Lord make his face to shine upon her and be gracious unto her, the Lord lift up his countenance upon her and give her peace.

Amen

The Lord's Prayer

The Lord be with you,
And with thy spirit,
Let us pray as Jesus has taught us:
Our Father who art in heaven, hallowed be Thy name, Thy kingdom come, Thy will be done, on earth as it is in heaven. Give us this day our daily bread, and forgive us our trespasses as we forgive those who trespass against us: And lead us not into temptation but deliver us from evil. For Thine is the kingdom, the power, and the glory forever and ever.

Amen.

Words of Assurance

O Almighty God, the God of the spirits of all flesh, who by a voice from did proclaim, Blessed are the dead who die in the Lord; Multiply, we beseech thee, to those who rest in Jesus the manifold blessings of thy love. That the good work, which thou didst begin in them, may be made perfect unto the day of Jesus Christ. And of thy mercy, O heavenly Father, grant that we, who serve thee on earth. may at last, together with them. Be partakers of the inheritance of the saints in light; for the sake of thy Son Jesus Christ our Lord.

Amen

Thanking Those who had Served but are Now Passed

Psalm 23 (Read Responsively) *Chaplain* / Congregation

The LORD is my shepherd; I shall not be in want.

He makes me lie down –in green pastures; and leads me beside still waters.

He revives my soul and guides me along right pathways for his name's sake.

Though I walk through the valley of the shadow of death, I shall fear no evil; for you are with me; your rod and your staff they comfort me.

You spread a table before me in the presence of those who trouble me;

You have anointed my head with oil; and my cup is running over.

Surely your goodness and mercy shall follow me all the days of my life;

ALL: And I will dwell in the house of the LORD forever.

John 10:14; Isaiah 40:11

Jesus said: I am the good shepherd. I know my own and my own know me. He will feed his flock like a shepherd; he will gather the lambs in his arms, and carry them in his bosom. The Word of the Lord!

Thanks be to God!

Going Forth in the Hope of God's Word

The God of peace, who brought again from the dead, out Lord Jesus Christ, the great Shepherd of the sheep, through the blood of the everlasting covenant; Make you perfect in every good work to do his will, working in you that which is pleasing in his sight; through Jesus Christ, to whom be the glory for ever and ever.

Amen

In the name of the Father, Son and Holy Spirit. *Amen*

Thanks: Giving and Receiving Gratitude for America's Troops

Memorial Day Service 2015

At Chapel of the Chimes, Hayward California
1300 on May 25, 2015

Adapted from the *Memorial Service, Interfaith Book of Worship for United States Forces 1974*

Bagpiper (Outside)

Prelude (Organ or Piano)

Bell Ringing

Color Guard: Proceeds placing flags, US and VFW on Narthex

Wreath for "Unknown Dead" is placed on altar

Invocation: VFW Chaplain

Thanking Those who had Served but are Now Passed

Hymn: "America the Beautiful"

Choir or Cantor: Sung in Hebrew (translation as follows)

From *The Union Prayer Book*, "Morning Service for the Festivals," 270:

> I have set the Lord always before me; surely God is at my right hand, I shall not be moved. Therefore my heart is glad and my glory rejoiceth; my flesh also dwelleth in safety. For Thou wilt not abandon my soul to the grave; neither wilt Thou suffer Thy faithful to see destruction. Thou makest me to know the path of life. In Thy presence is fullness of joy, at Thy right hand, bliss for evermore.

Reading from *The Union Prayer Book*, 271

> Thou who reigns in Heaven! The solemn call of this hour revives within our memories the beloved who have passed through the portal of death . . . . Now, as in the hour when they laid off the raiment of mortality, our hearts yearn for them. Precious links binding heart to heart still are broken. Transfigured by memory, our dear ones stand again before in this sacred hour we remember them with gratitude and a benediction.

Song or Chant and Prayer (Buddhist or Native American)

Address: "Simon's Service" by Chaplain (Capt) Edgar S Welty, Jr., United States Volunteers/America

Prayer of St. Francis-Catholic Priest

> Lord, make me an instrument of your peace,
> Where there is hatred, let me sow love;
> where there is injury, pardon;
> where there is doubt, faith;
> where there is despair, hope;

Thanks: Giving and Receiving Gratitude for America's Troops

where there is darkness, light;
where there is sadness, joy;

O Divine Master, grant that I may not so much seek to be consoled as to console; to be understood as to understand; to be loved as to love.

For it is in giving that we receive;
it is in pardoning that we are pardoned;
and it is in dying that we are born to eternal life.

Last Post (Bugler)

Period of Silence

The Suffrages:

Many people die by violence, war, and famine each day: Show your mercy to those who suffer so unjustly these sins against your love, and gather them to your eternal realm of peace. We pray to our Creator.
God hear our prayer.
Many friends and members of our families have gone before us and await your realm: Grant them an everlasting home with you. We pray to our Sustainer
God hear our prayer.
That those in public office may promote justice and peace/ We pray to our Savior.
God hear our prayer.
For all of service men and women currently on active duty, especially in the Middle East and Afganistan: Please keep them safe. We pray in the the name of the prophets.
God hear our prayer.
For veterans everywhere: May they be blessed for the sacrifices they have made in the cause of freedom. We pray to the Ground of all Being.
God hear our prayer.

Thanking Those who had Served but are Now Passed

Reveille Bugler

Ode of Remembrance

Hymn: "God Be With You."

Red Poppy Drop with "Taps" Bulger and then with "Amazing Grace" on the Bagpipes

Benediction: Chaplain

Postlude: Organ or Piano with Bagpipes "Going Home"

Appendix

A Speech by President Obama

OBAMA, BARRACK AS SENATOR from "Red State, Blue State Speech"

". . . It's what allows us to pursue our individual dreams, yet still come together as a single American family: "E pluribus unum," out of many, one.

Now even as we speak, there are those who are preparing to divide us, the spin masters and negative ad peddlers who embrace the politics of anything goes.

Well, I say to them tonight, there's not a liberal America and a conservative America; there's the United States of America.

There's not a black America and white America and Latino America and Asian America; there's the United States of America.

The pundits, the pundits like to slice and dice our country into red states and blue States: red states for Republicans, blue States for Democrats. But I've got news for them, too. We worship an awesome God in the blue states, and we don't like federal agents poking around our libraries in the red states.

We coach little league in the blue states and, yes, we've got some gay friends in the red states.

There are patriots who opposed the war in Iraq, and there are patriots who supported the war in Iraq.

We are one people, all of us pledging allegiance to the stars and stripes, all of us defending the United States of America. "

Appendix

Personal Expanded Translation of Matthew 4:25–5:1-2; 12-17

Chapter 4

25. And many crowds followed him...

Chapter 5

1. But seeing the crowds, Jesus went up into the mountain, and seating Himself, (Taking a position of teaching authority), His disciples came near to Him.
2. And opening His mouth, taught them saying: Blessed are the...

12. Rejoice and leap for joy, for you reward is great in Heaven;...
13. You are the salt of the earth, (a symbol of purity, an agent of preservation and a means to give zest to life); but if the salt (you and your faith community) becomes tasteless (loses your qualities of purity, preservation and favor) with what shall those attributes be restored? For it has value for nothing anymore, but to be thrown out and to be trampled under by the crowds.
14. You (as a faithful community) are set up as God's beacon to the world. No way, if you think of your community as a) city (with walls and towers) set on a mount (defensible high ground above the tree line) can you be hidden. (You may shine to God's glory or be a shameful display of divine judgment.)
15. Nor do they light a lamp and put under the grain measure, (or worse yet under the bed where it would set the mattress ablaze) but on the lamp-stand; and it shines for all who are in the house.
16. So let you light shine before men, so they may see your good works, and may glorify your Father who is in Heaven.
17. Do not think I came to annul the law

Appendix

Based largely on:
Green, Jay P Sr., The Interlinear Greek-English NEW TESTAMENT: With Strong's Concordance numbers Above Each Word, (This is Volume IV of The Interlinear Hebrew-Greek-English-Bible.) 2nd.and Revised Edition, 1984, Hendrickson Publishers, USA

With insights from:
    Barclay, William, The Gospel of Matthew, Volume1, Daily Study Bible Series, Revised Ed. Westminster Press, 1975, Philadelphia and
    Strong, James, Strong's Exhaustive Concordance of the Bible, Abington Press, 1980, Nashville TN

Resources

Articles

DeCosse, David, *Totaling Up; It was an Unjust War (2ⁿᵈ US/Iraqi War)*, Markkula.
Center for Applied Ethics, Santa Clara University, Silicon Valley, CA.
Druck, Ken, *True Patriotism: It Goes Beyond Politics*, Page B7. *San Diego Union/Tribune*, July 4, 2014.
Mageun, Shira, PhD. & Litz, Brett, PhD, *Moral Injury in Veterans of War*, PTSD Research Quarterly, Vol. 23 #1, 2012.
Rigstad, Mark, *Jus Ad Bellum* After 9/11: A State of the Art Report, Oakland University.
Ritchie, Elspeth Cameron, *Moral Injury: "A Profound Sense of Alienation and Abject Shame"*, Time, April 17, 2013.
Tolstoy, Leo, *A Letter to a Hindu*. Project Gutenberg, 2004.
Welty, Edgar Shirley Sr., *Communism: What and Why*, editorial essay from "The Voice" published in the U. S. *Congressional Record* August 10, 1954.

Book and eBooks

Albright, W.F. and Mann, C. S., *The Anchor Bible: Matthew*, Doubleday 1971 New York, NY.
Anderson, Gregory, *Love. Violence and the Cross: How the Nonviolent God Saves Us Through the Cross of Jesus*, Cascade Publications, 2010, Eugene OR.
Anderson, Ken, *Where to Find It in the Bible*, Thomas Nelson, 2001, Nashville TN.
Atherton, Mark, *Celts and Christians: New Approaches to the Religious Traditions of Britain and Ireland*, University of Wales, 2002, Cardiff GB.
Augsburger, *The Communicators' Commentary Mastering the New Testament, Volume 1, Matthew*, Word, 2012, USA.
Bainton, Roland, *Christian Attitudes towards War and Peace, from* 1961, Abington Press 15ᵗʰ Printing 1986, Nashville.

Resources

Blenkinsopp, Joseph, *A History of Prophecy in Israel: From the Settlement of the Land to the Hellenistic Period*, West Minister Press, 1983, Philadelphia, PA.

Bawer, Bruce, *Stealing Jesus*, Three Rivers Press, 1997, New York, NY.

Barclay, William, *The Gospel of Matthew, Volume1, Daily Study Bible Series*, Revised Ed. Westminster Press, 1975, Philadelphia.

Brandon, S. G. F., *The Trial of Jesus of Nazareth*, Palidin, 1971, London.

Brock, Rita & Lettina, Gabriella, *Soul Repair: Recovering From Moral Injury after War*, Beacon Press, 2012, Boston, 2012.

Bruce, *Hard Saying of Jesus, How Fundamentalism Betrays Christianity*, InterVarsity Press, 1983, Downers Grove, IL.

Bunyan John, *The Pilgrim's Progress*, edited by Helms Hal M. Paraclete Press, 1992, Orleans, Massachusetts.

Calvin, John, *Institutes of the Christian Religion*, Westminster Press, 1960, Philadelphia.

Carroll, Andrew, *Grace Under Fire: Letters of Faith in Times of War*, WaterBrook Press, 2007, Colorado Springs, CO.

Carter, Jimmy, *Living Faith*, Times Books, 1996, New York, NY.

Carter, Stephen L., *God's Name in Vain: The Wrongs and Rights of Religion in Politics*, Basic Books, 2000, New York, NY.

Cesaretti, C. A. and Vitale, Joseph T., *Rumors of War: A Moral and Theological Perspective on the Arms Race*, Seabury Press 1982, New York, NY.

Chittister, Joan, *In Search of Belief, Revised Edition*, Liguori/Triumph, Liguor, MO.

Dark, David, *The Gospel According to America: A meditation on God-Blessed, Christ-haunted Idea*, Westminster John Knox Press, 2005, Louisville KY.

Doke, Joseph J., *M.K. Gandhi: An Indian Patriot in South Africa*, Madras. G.A. Natesan & Co., 1919.

Durant, William *Caesar and Christ: A History of Roman Civilization and of Christianity from their Beginnings to A.D. 325*, Simon and Schuster, 1944, New York, NY.

Farrelly, M. John, *The Trinity: Rediscovering the Central Christian Mystery*, Rowman & Littlefield Publishers Inc. 2005, Lanham, MY.

Ferguson, Duncan S., *Biblical Hermeneutics*, John Knox Press, 1986, Atlanta, GA.

Finkel, David, *Thank You for Your Service*, Sarah Crichton Books Farrar, Straus and Giroux, 2013, New York, NY.

Fotion, N. and Elfstrom, G., *Military Ethics: Guidelines for Peace and War*, Routledge & Kegan Paul, 1986, Boston, MA.

Freedman, David Noel, *Anchor Bible Dictionary in Six Volumes*, Doubleday, 1992, New York, NY.

Fry, Ruth, *Victories without Violence*, Ocean Tree/Liberty, 1986, Santa Fe. NM.

Gandhi, Mahatma, *An Autobiography or the Story of My Experiments with Truth*, Beacon Press, 1957, Boston, MA.

Gandhi, Mahatma, *Ruskin UNTO THIS LAST: A Paraphrase*, Navajivan Publishing House, 2007, Ahmedabad, INDIA.

Resources

Good, Jack, *The Dishonest Church*, Rising Star Press, 2003, Scots Valley, CA.

Green, Jay P Sr., *The Interlinear Greek-English NEW TESTAMENT: With Strong's Concordance numbers Above Each Word, (This is Volume IV of The Interlinear Hebrew-Greek-English-Bible.)* 2nd.and Revised Edition, 1984, Hendrickson Publishers, USA.

Guastad, Edwin Scot, *A Religious History of America*, New Revised Edition, Harper 1990, San Francisco, CA.

Harmony House, *The Holy Bible: Old and New Testaments in the Authorized King James Version*, Harmony House, 1977, New York, NY.

Hart, Thomas N., *The Art of Christian Listening*, Paulist Press, 1980, Ramsey, NY.

Hayes, John H. & Holladay, Carl R. *Biblical Exegesis: A Beginner's Handbook*, John Knox Press, 1987, Atlanta, GA.

Herman, Judith Lewis, *Trauma and Recovery: The Aftermath of Violence from Domestic Abuse to Political Terror*, 1992, Basic Books.

Johnson, Daniel R., *The Greatest Soldier Who Ever Lived*, Providence Publicans, Kokomo, IN.

Jones, Alexander, *The Jerusalem Bible* 1966, Doubleday and Company, Inc. Garden City, NY.

Jones, Serene, *Trauma and Grace: Theology in a Ruptured World*, 2009, Westminster, John Knox.

Jones, Stanley, *Mahatma Gandhi-An Interpretation*, Stone and Pierce, 1968.

Josephus, *The Jewish War*, Revised Edition, Penguin Classics, 1970, London.

Kerr, Hugh T., *The Simple Gospel: Reflections on Christian Faith*, Westminster/ John Knox Press, 1991, Louisville, KY.

Killen, Patricia O'Connell DeBeer, John, *The Art of Theological Reflection* 1994. Copy right 2000 Printing, Crossroad Publishing, New York, NY.

Kubo, *A Reader's Greek –English Lexicon of the New Testament*, Zondervan Publishing House, 1975, Grand Rapids, MI.

Lippy, Charles H. etal, *Christianity comes to the Americas 1492-1776*, Paragon House, 1992, New York, NY.

Lieu, Judith etal, *The Jews among Pagans and Christians in the Roman Empire*, Routledge, 1992, London.

Lockman Foundation, *The New American Standard Bible*, Foundation Press, 1971, La Habra, CA.

Love, Gregory Anderson, *Love, Violence and the Cross: How the Nonviolent God Saves Us through the Cross of Christ*, Cascade Books, 1965, Eugene OR.

Maddow, Rachel; *Drift: The Unmooring of American Military Power*, Crown Books, 2012, New York, NY.

Metzer, Bruce M. and Murphy, Roland E. *The New Oxford Annotated Bible with the Apocryphal/ Deuterocanonical Book: New Revised Standard Version*, Oxford University Press, 1991, New York, NY.

Resources

Metzer, Bruce M. and Coogan, Michael D., *The Oxford Companion to the Bible*, Oxford University Press, 1993, New York, NY.
Miller, J Maxwell and Hayes, John H., *A History of Ancient Israel and Judah*, Westminster Press, 1986, Philadelphia.
More, Thomas, *Care of the Soul: A Guide for Cultivating Depth and Sacredness in Everyday Life*, Harper Collins, 1967, New York, NY.
Morrison, Clinton, *An Analytical Concordance to the Revised Standard Version of the Bible*, Westminster Press, 1979, Philadelphia.
Murthy, B. Srinivasa, *Mahatma Gandhi and Leo Tolstoy Letters*, Long Beach Publications, 1987, Long Beach, CA.
National Council of Churches, *Holy Bible, Revised Standard Version*, Collins Clear Type Press, 1946, 1952, New York, NY.
Nave, Orville J. Revised by Coder, S. Maxwell, *Nave Topical Bible: A Digest of the Holy Scriptures*, Moody Press, 1974, Chicago, IL
Nestle and Aland, *Novum Testamentum Graece*, Deutsche Bibelgesellschaft, 1979, Stuttgart, West Germany.
Office of the General Assembly (Presbyterian Church {USA}, *Is Christ Divided?* 1988.
Office of the General Assembly, *Presbyterian Understanding and Use of Holy Scripture: Position Statement of the General Assembly Presbyterian Church (U.S.A.)*, 1979, New York, NY.
Prather, Stephen, *Religious Literacy: What Every American Needs to Know and Doesn't*: Harper Collins, 2007, San Francisco.
Richardson, Alan, *A Theological Word of the Bible*, Macmillan.
Rogers, Jack B. and McKim, Donald K. *The Authority and Interpretation of the Bible: A Historical Approach*, Harper and Row, Publishers, 1978, San Francisco, CA.
Rogers, Jack B., *Claiming the Center: Churches and Conflicting Worldviews*, Westminster/ John Knox 1995, Louisville, KY.
Ruskin, John, *Unto This Last*, Grant Educational Co. LTD, 1921, Glasgow, GB.
Ryrie, Charles Caldwell, *The Ryrie Study Bible: New King James Version*, Moody 1985, Chicago.
Santhanam, K., Author Editors Munshi, K. M. & Diwakar, R. R., *The Gospel of Gandhi*, Sharatiya Vidya Shavan, 1967, Bombay, India.
Sardar, Ziauddin and Davies, Merryl Wyn, *Why Do People Hate America?* Disinformation Company Ltd. 2002 New York, NY.
Shannon, Thomas A. *Catholic Perspectives on Peace and War*, Rowland and Littlefield Publishers Inc., 2003, Lanham, NY.
Strong, James, *Strong's Exhaustive Concordance of the Bible*, Abington Press, 1980, Nashville, TN.
Swaim, J. Carter, *War, Peace. and the Bible*, Orbis Books, 1983, Maryknoll, NY.
Swartley, Willard M., *Israel's Scripture Traditions and the Synoptic Gospels: Story Shaping Story*, 1994, Hendrickson Publishers, Inc., Peabody, and Massachusetts.

Resources

Time, *Great Events of the 20th.Century*, Time Books, 1997, New York, NY.
Tolstoy, Leo, *Christ's Christianity*, Kegan Paul, Trench & Co., 1885, London, GB.
Tolstoy Leo, *A Confession of What I Believe*, Oxford University Press, 1940, London, GB.
Tolstoy, Leo, *The Kingdom of God is within You*, Noonday, 1961, London, GB.
Tolstoy, Leo, *Lift up Your Eyes,* Julian Press, 1960, New York, NY.
Tolstoy, Leo, *My Religion*, Thomas Y. Crowell & Co., New York, NY.
Tolstoy, Leo, *The Only Commandment*, Westminster Press, 1962.
Turse, Nick, *Kill Everything that Moves*, The Real War in Vietnam, Metropolitan Books, New York, NY.
United States Department of Defense, *Korea Reborn: A Grateful Nation Honors War Veterans for Sixty Years of Growth*, Remember My Service Productions, 2013 , Seoul, South Korea.
Volf, Miroslav, *The End of Memory: Remembering Rightly in a Violent World*, 2006, Eerdmans, Norton.
Vonnegut, Kurt, *Armageddon in Retrospect*, G.P. Putnam's Sons, 2008 New York, NY.
Wallis, Jim, *Agenda for Biblical People: A New Focus for Developing a Life-Style of Discipleship*, Harper and Row, 1962, New York, NY.
Wallis, Jim, *God's Politics: Why the Right Gets It Wrong and the Left Doesn't Get It*, Harper Collins, 2005, San Francisco, CA.
Wuthnow, Robert, *The Struggle for America' Soul: Evangelicals, Liberals and Secularism*, William B. Eerdmans Publishing Company, 1989, Grand Rapids, MI.
Young, William P., *The Shack: A Novel*, Windblown Media, 2007, Los Angeles, CA.
Zikmund, Barbara Brown (Editor) *The Living Theological Heritage of the United Church of Christ, Volume Three*, Hambrick-Stowe, Charles Colonial and National Beginnings, Pilgrim Press, 1998, Cleveland, OH.
Zweig, Stefan, *The Living Thoughts of Tolstoy*, Fawcett Publications, 1963 Greenwich GB.

Consultants

Dean Polly Coote, *Biblical Greek*
Professor/Psychologist R. Scot Sullender, PhD. *Dynamics of Trauma*

Films with Topics

Documentary Film *1862*	Historical Perspective on PTSD
Documentary Film *"Devils in Baggy Pants"*	Combat WW2
Documentary Film *Salinger*	Alienation Post WW2

Resources

Documentary film, *Telephone Crisis Line, Veterans Press One*	Suicide
Feature Film, *American Sniper*	Cold-blooded Killing
Feature Film *Apocalypse Now*	Warrior gone "Bad"
Feature Film *The Best Years of Our Lives*	Wasted time WW2
Feature Film *Dances with Wolves*	F**k this s**t, Let me die
Feature Film *Doctor Strangelove*	MAD war-planners
Feature Film *Flags of Our Fathers*	Selling war
Feature Film *Gandhi*	Power of Nonviolence
Feature Film, *Hurt Locker*	The "Rush" of combat
Feature Film *Jacob's Ladder*	After-life
Feature Film *Letters from Iwo Jima*	Explaining to the "Home-front"
Feature Film *The Longest Day*	Massive military machine in motion
Feature Film *The Man in the Gray Flannel Suit*	A cog in the machine
Feature Film *The Messenger*	Notification of Next of Kin
Feature Film *Platoon*	Small unit dynamics
Feature Film *Saving Private Ryan*	One man vs. the mission
Feature Film *Taps*	Worship of death
Feature Film *Tribes*	World of military vs. other
Feature Film *Unbroken*	Endurance
Feature Film *War Games*	Uncontrollability of war

Speeches, Sermons

Church, Forrest. *Great Lecture Library: A City on a Hill.*
Kennedy, John. *Speech as President-Elect.*
Lincoln, Abraham. *Second Inagural Address.*
Obama, Barrack. *Red State, Blue State Speech.*
Regan, Ronald. *Farewell Address.*
Thomas, John. *Taking Scripture Seriously.*
Washington, George. *Farewell Address.*
Winthrop, John. *A Model of Christian Charity.*

Telephone

Veterans' Crisis Line: 1 (800) 273 8255, Press 1

Websites

After Deployment: afterdeployment.org
AHEC Digital Library: library.ncahec.net
American Legion: legion.org

Resources

Coaching into Care: mirecc.va.gov/coaching
Department of Veterans Affairs (VA) and Department of Defense (DoD) Clinical Practice Guideline for the Management of Post-Traumatic Stress: www.healthquality>va.gov/ptsd/ptsd_full.pdf
Disabled American Veterans: dav.org
Employment Services: www.acp-advisornet.org
Homelessness, National Alliance to End: www.endhomelessness.org
International Critical Incident Stress Foundation: www.icisf.org
International Society for Traumatic Stress Studies-Dedicated to trauma treatment, Education and Research: www.istss.org
Joint Services Support: jointservicessupport.org
Make The Connection: MakeTheConnection.net
Military Home Front: militaryhomefront.dod.mil
Military One Source: militaryonesource.mil
National Guard: nationalgurad.mil
National Center for Post-Traumatic Stress Disorder-Provides many useful resources on the issue of PTSD: www.ptsd.va.gov
National Institute of Mental Health: www.nimh,nih.gov
National Coalition for Homeless Veterans: nchv.org
PD Health: pdhealth.mil
Post Traumatic Stress Syndrome: ptsd.va.gov
Real Warriors: realwarriors.net
Secular Recovery Program: www.unhooked.com
Substance Abuse and Mental Health Services Administration: www.samhsa.gov
Swords to plowshares: swords-to-plowshares.org
United Service Organization: uso.org
VA Information: MakeTheConnection.net
VA Web Site: va.gov
Veterans Crisis Line: VeteransCrisisLine.net
Veterans of Foreign Wars: vfw.org
Veterans' Writing Project-Journal: www.O-Dark-Thirty.org
WarWithin: WarWithin.org

www.ingramcontent.com/pod-product-compliance
Lightning Source LLC
Chambersburg PA
CBHW050832160426
43192CB00010B/1992